"Being Catholic in an imperfect world comes with its own unique set of challenges. Whether you encounter rebellious teens, unsupportive extended family, mental illness, a contentious marriage, or other crises of faith, morality, and psychology, *When Faith Causes Family Friction* has just what you need. In his usual no-nonsense, practical, and humorous style, Dr. Ray Guarendi offers wisdom and insight from an authentically Catholic perspective and with the voice of experience. An easy, entertaining, and enlightening read for Catholics from all walks of life!"

—Danielle Bean, publisher, *Catholic Digest,* and author, *Momnipotent*

"Dr. Ray Guarendi combines his keen intellect, his years of experience as a clinical psychologist, and his hands-on experience as a father of ten to create a book that is as wise as it is warm. *When Faith Causes Family Friction* is a must-read book for anyone who faces the daunting task of evangelizing to the toughest crowd of all: your own family."

—Jennifer Fulwiler, author, *Something Other Than God*

"Most Catholics have no problem practicing their faith...while they're still in church. Once Mass is over, however, it gets much more challenging. In his book *When Faith Causes Family Friction*, Dr. Ray Guarendi addresses several of the most common difficulties that arise from living the Catholic faith at home, in the workplace, and in the real world. In a clear and succinct manner (with lots of humor thrown in), he tells us what we need to know in order to really *live* our faith 24/7. Highly recommended!"

—Gary Zimak, speaker and author, *Faith, Hope, and Clarity*

"Dr. Ray has done it again! His list of snappy (but charitable) answers to rude questions is worth the price of the book. But there's so much more."

—Mike Aquilina, author, *Yours Is the Church*

"Dr. Ray gives practical spiritual advice while answering tough questions concerning raising children in the faith. A true guidebook of responses and actions to help parents and grandparents persevere in love while maintaining and passing on truth."

—Julie Dortch Cragon, author, *Amazing Graces:
The Blessings of Sacramentals*

"Who wouldn't benefit from a healthy dose of Dr. Ray? His simple, straightforward insights are an antidote to the friction and the frazzle in our families. Clear, concrete guidance for the confused. Faithful, funny direction for the distraught. And just plain good advice for Catholic parents of all shapes and sizes. Thanks, Dr. Ray. I needed that!"

—Gina Loehr, author *Saint Francis, Pope Francis*

"Do you get upset about faith related conflicts with your family and friends? Dr. Ray's book is the best I've ever read about such problems. It is not only inspiring but also sensible and humorous. You will find surprising answers to questions you thought there were no answers for."

—Ronda Chervin, Ph.D., professor of philosophy
at Holy Apostles College and Seminary

"This book is down to earth, practical, funny, and a breath of fresh air. Thanks Dr. Ray, from a father of nine!"

—Chris Padgett, coauthor, *Holy Marriage, Happy Marriage*

When Faith Causes Family Friction

Dr. Ray Tackles the Tough Questions

DR. RAY GUARENDI

servant

AN IMPRINT OF
FRANCISCAN MEDIA
Cincinnati, Ohio

Scripture passages have been taken from the *Revised Standard Version*, Catholic edition. Copyright 1946, 1952, 1971 by the Division of Christian Education of the National Council of Churches of Christ in the USA. Used by permission. All rights reserved. Quotes are taken from the English translation of the *Catechism of the Catholic Church* for the United States of America (indicated as *CCC*), 2nd ed. Copyright 1997 by United States Catholic Conference—Libreria Editrice Vaticana.

Cover and book design by Mark Sullivan
Cover image © iStockphoto | wabeno

LIBRARY OF CONGRESS CATALOGING-IN-PUBLICATION DATA
Guarendi, Ray.
When faith causes family friction : Dr. Ray tackles the tough questions / Dr. Ray Guarendi.
pages cm
Includes bibliographical references and index.
ISBN 978-1-61636-923-1 (paperback : acid-free paper)
1. Families—Religious aspects—Catholic Church—Miscellanea. 2. Christian life—Miscellanea. I. Title.
BX2351.G83 2015
248.4—dc23
2015007939
ISBN 978-1-61636-923-1

Published by Servant, an imprint of Franciscan Media.
28 W. Liberty St.
Cincinnati, OH 45202
www.FranciscanMedia.org

Printed in the United States of America.
Printed on acid-free paper.
15 16 17 18 19   5 4 3 2

Contents

Introduction

"Clinical psychologist" is my professional title. My early education in the field could rightly be called secular. That is, the ideas and perspectives I heard were those standard in a nonreligious university program. My instructors pretty much avoided matters touching on traditional religion and morals. While acknowledging that many clients did live by some religion, they advised us to maintain a dogmatically neutral moral stance. Though I practiced my Catholic faith back then, I would practice psychology as I was taught.

Some years after graduating, I drifted from the Church. I didn't head toward hostile anti-religion, saying, "Christian beliefs are pre–psychological enlightenment." Rather, I took a more self-affirming attitude: God sees things in the same ways that I do.

Thank God, he doesn't. By his mercy and over several years, I scratched and clawed my way back into the Church. While I still practiced psychology with the general population, more Christians began seeking my guidance. They trusted that I would understand and respect their deepest held beliefs. It was a trust they were finding less and less elsewhere.

Matters of faith and psychology routinely intersect. Parenting, emotions, anxieties, relationships—all intersect with the most profound question for religious people: How can I live my faith better, in thought and action, especially within my family?

Most Christians try to live within a faith-based set of beliefs and morals. And they ask questions wrapped around their beliefs. This book collects the most frequent of these questions that I am asked regarding issues of faith and family. How do I get my kids, and myself, to be more attentive at Mass? Why are my children resisting the faith? Why did my children leave the Church when they became adults? How do I best respond to my family's criticisms of my religion? How do I protect my children's innocence in a culture that morally disagrees with me? What do I say to loved ones whose thinking about religion is confused? What do I do when my spouse is threatened by my faith?

Some of these questions I've grappled with personally. I suspect you have, too. That's why I'm writing this book. I hope you will find here some advice to help you "run with perseverance the race that is set before us" (Hebrews 12:1).

Mass Resistance

God has given us the Mass for our infinite well-being. It is good for us in the short-term—life here—and for the long-term—life in heaven.

This does not mean that everyone will understand the value of the Mass. Just because something is for our immeasurable benefit doesn't mean we will want it. Some wayward children resist the arms of the loving Father.

A Choice for Life

Dear Dr. Ray,

My daughter, age fourteen, is starting to resist going to church. I worry that if I force her, someday she'll reject religion altogether. My mother tells me not to push her, that as she gets older, she'll come around.

—*Waiting*

Here's a child-rearing experiment: From age two forward, do not make a child do anything against her will. Twinkies or lima beans—her choice. School or television—her preference. Hug her brother or smack him—whatever. She can eat what she wants, sleep when she wants, work how she wants, and visit your mother if she wants.

With each year, will your child choose more good and reject more bad? Or will she develop into a self-absorbed, unhealthy young adult?

Kids aren't naturally inclined toward everything that is in their best interest. (Who is?) If they were, how much guidance would they need? The whole growing-up process would be far less demanding, for big and little. Loving parents use force—not physical but social and moral. They make a child, when necessary, do what she resists and not do what she seeks.

A television show once asked me to be a guest for this topic: Should parents force their values upon their children, or should they be free to choose their own? It didn't take a shrink to analyze the show's bias.

Your mother seems to be echoing a similar sentiment. (Do you think she watched the show?) That is, one must feel like acting for the act to be genuine. If it is imposed from the outside, little settles inside. The roots are shallow, easily pulled up.

Some believe this to be especially true for faith in God. Teaching anything religious is psychologically acceptable as long as a child remains open, but once she resists, religious instruction borders on compulsion. Using such logic, passing on any values would be dependent upon a child's cooperative feelings.

I'll confess, as a forward-looking third-grader, I had little inner push to master the multiplication tables. Mrs. Becker made me, backed by my parents' unspoken demand.

Must a parent watch and wait until a young person somehow feels a longing for God? While some children do seek a divine connection on their own, they are a minority. The majority of God seekers are introduced to him early in life, by faith-filled parents, and come to know him more deeply with time and exposure.

Is free choice a fair choice? If your daughter will one day leave the faith, shouldn't she understand what she will be leaving? If you allow her to learn by herself, she could remain in youthful ignorance, which may grow into arrogant ignorance. True freedom begins with knowing what is good.

Teens, as well as many grown-ups, have little or no idea of the possible consequences of a bad decision. It is infinitely unwise to allow the youthful to decide independently about a matter of infinite importance. And what decision is more core to existence than that of moving toward God or away from him?

A tragic reality fuels today's parents' anxiety over their children's faith journey: the large numbers of adults who jettison the faith of their childhood. Many of the "fallen away" proclaim, "I was made to go to church as a kid, and as I got older, I wanted to decide for myself." Decades of doing therapy have taught me that many, if not most of us, are routinely unaware of our true motives. "I was made to" is often the spoken rationale for the unspoken "I don't want to anymore." Later rejection has little to do with being forced to attend Mass years earlier.

Throughout my teens, my mother insisted I visit my ninety-plus-year-old great-aunt, an activity near the bottom of my boyhood to-do list. Did she thus risk making me one day shun old people? I don't think she ever worried about that. Or did she show me a side of life I needed to see and wouldn't look at on my own? Long after I had Mom as my motivator, I not only continued visits with the elderly but came to appreciate them.

A father told me his teens wanted to sleep in on Sunday mornings rather than go to Mass. Dad wouldn't hear of it. He knew that at Mass, something could somehow touch their souls. One thing for sure: That would not happen if they weren't there.

Dependent Independence

Dear Dr. Ray,
My twenty-year-old son has returned home from college for the summer and is arguing that he is old enough to decide whether or not to attend Mass. He also tells us he has pretty much stopped going to Mass at school.
—*Still the Parent*

Age entitlement: It's the juvenile mind-set that proclaims, "I'm (enter number), so I can (enter perk—date, drive, dress as I wish, buy what I want, and so on)." Blossoming autonomy incorporates a slew of so-called freedoms that are supposed to arrive just because a certain age does. Some of these freedoms might arrive— if the child-turned-adult buys his own car, covers his own rent, pays his own bills. In short, if he is really and truly independent.

Your son may have the illusion of full self-determination because, for the better part of the last year or so, he's been playing house at school. But the reality is stubborn: He is still reliant upon your support. Despite what he believes, there are limits to his autonomy, and some of those limits are set by you.

College kids drift from Mass for a range of reasons: a general questioning of the faith (for upward of half of kids, statistics say), an apathy toward things religious, freedom to party late Saturday and sleep late Sunday, a newfound status of adulthood: "I'm a big boy now, so no more guidance, thank you."

Whatever your son's thinking, your thinking remains the same: Mass is nonnegotiable. It is a given of his summer relocation status. Otherwise, the perks of young adulthood (no doubt supported in whole or in part by you)—car, computer, cell phone, insurance, and so on—will be reassessed accordingly. At which your son may conclude he went from Disney World to Alcatraz in one short day in May.

If you mandate Mass for your son, are you asking for further resistance? (Refer back to the previous chapter, "A Choice for Life.") Could he resent being treated as if he's still a child?

Perhaps. A young adult living at home does make some rules trickier to enforce. Nonetheless, parenting any-aged children often comes down to taking a stance. Your stance: Our family worships God, and Mass is at the center of our worship.

OK, so your son is in church, but his mind isn't. It is back at school, where he is supposedly free. While you can't do much to stop his mind from journeying, you can make sure his body stays in a holy place. And who knows, every so often his mind and body might connect, giving the grace of Mass a chance to reach him.

Now, if you decide to let him decide about Mass, consider: Will your decision be for your son alone? Or will younger siblings be watching, and will they conclude that core family standards relax with age? No matter where they live when they reach their brother's age, will they too think they've earned the right to choose for or against Mass?

Regarding your son's campus liberty, here your influence dwindles. He may be miles beyond your eye- and earshot. Your knowledge of his whereabouts and conduct is mostly indirect: grades, billing statements, conduct reports—do institutions do those anymore? Do you have a ten-year-old daughter who can tail your son and send back daily accounts?

Rather than regularly questioning your son, admit your limits. Acknowledge that you can't monitor his Sundays, or any days on campus for that matter. To the degree, however, that you provide tuition, cell phone, car, or cash, you do have long-range leverage. Your financial help is not automatic but is linked to his honesty and reliability. His promise—and proof—of attending Mass is a small exchange for all the goodies you still dispense, at home and away.

One father found a creative way to confirm his son's Sunday itinerary. He told him, "The first time I pick you up from school, I'm going to visit the parish priest and ask if he knows you."

Touchy Topic

Dear Dr. Ray,
My twenty-three-year-old daughter slowly drifted away from Mass after she moved out on her own. Our relationship is good, but whenever I bring up the subject, she shuts down. What can I say to persuade her?
—Stifled

I can say what not to say: "Did you get to Mass this week?" "Father has been asking where you've been." "The priest at Holy Family near you gives great homilies—and they have donuts after Mass." "When was the last time you saw the inside of a church?"

Let's begin with what we know. You gave your daughter a belief system, one that you embrace to this day. She understands exactly your thinking. She lived with it for over two decades, and you've reiterated it many times since she moved out. Your conversations don't end well. (And you thought her eye rolls would stop with her teen years.)

Now let's speculate. Perhaps your daughter hasn't abandoned her belief in God or the Church. Instead she has decided that being at Mass isn't necessary in order for her to be a good person or even a faithful one. Mass has become a negotiable among her religious choices. Her independence now allows her the freedom to set her own schedule, and weekends are social time. Put another way, church has become one place to visit among many.

Some adolescent rebellion may be lingering, meaning she sees the faith as something she has, however temporarily, outgrown. It was something you both shared when she was little, but she's a big girl now.

Your best persuasion is a good relationship. You have that, and you want to keep it. Continuing to broach a sore subject may only make it sorer. I suspect your daughter doesn't like feeling on edge, waiting for you to guide the conversation around to her religious shortcomings.

Don't try to be subtle: "The parish is having a spaghetti dinner next Saturday after Mass. We can go to Mass first and then eat." Or, "So what do you do now that your Sunday mornings are open?" "Your cousin has returned to church, and she seems so much happier."

What drives a parent to keep visiting a topic that gets rawer with each visit? A number of factors.

The heavy stakes factor. This is not about what school to attend, what job to seek, or what car to buy—all of which are transient decisions with transient consequences. The faith decision reaches to the very ends of life. Thus the desperation to steer a child back on course. If she rejects Mass, what will fall next? The matter is deemed too urgent to leave silent.

The failure factor. "How did I fail to impart the faith?" "What did I miss?" "What could I have done better?"

As we'll see in more detail later, such self-blame can be badly misdirected. Nonetheless, it can mercilessly corrode a parent's peace, compelling her to keep pushing even though a young adult pushes back harder.

The rejection factor. "How can she turn away from something that was once such a big part of who she was? At one time she wanted to be a nun."

Because the reversal seems so incomprehensible, it can't be totally real. It must be a phase, a temporary grab for independence. Perhaps. But for the present, for whatever reasons, the child-turned-adult has shifted her mind-set. The more you're convinced, "She just needs to be nudged to come back to who she is," the harder you'll nudge when she doesn't budge.

Hope will help you hold your tongue. A good percentage of young adults raised in the Church stay in the Church or return some time after leaving. One survey found that up to 80 percent of those taken to church as children attend church in adulthood. That's a sky-high success rate for anything involving free will.

So do you avoid the subject altogether? Yes and no. Yes in that you don't initiate it anymore. Don't advise, push, or argue. The time for that has passed.

No, in that, if your daughter brings it up, listen and hear her out. Your aim is to get inside her head and understand her. Let her explain her thinking. Who knows, hearing herself, she may come to realize she's not sounding so enlightened.

Brace yourself for what you might hear. Don't panic. Remember, she is twenty-three. Do you think now as you did when you were twenty-three?

Missing in Action

Dear Dr. Ray,

My husband is a good father but seldom attends church with the family. My twelve-year-old son is asking, "Why do I have to go to church if Dad doesn't?"

—*The Sunday Parent*

If you're asking me how to answer your son, let me ask you, "What do you think I am—a psychologist or something?"

Actually I am, so I suspect your son's motive is not what he says it is. I've learned that anything—or anyone—can be a justification for something you really don't want to do. If your son is ambivalent toward church—not all that uncommon for his age—Dad may be the most convenient rationale.

Why do I believe your son is coopting his father for his purposes? For one thing, if he really wanted to attend Mass, if he were convinced of its worth, he would attend no matter what Dad did. For another, he'd probably push Dad to go with him. At this point though, he's asking, "If this is so important, why doesn't Dad think so?" He presents the parent vote as tied at one to one.

No doubt, a faithful father is a powerful presence, especially for a son. He states, in word and action, that religion is not solely a woman's thing. Still, even if Dad's faith walk is a stumble, you can steadfastly walk your child toward God. Though two parents on the same spiritual page is the ideal, one parent living in faith is far better than none doing so.

So how do you steady your walk? Explain your husband to your son. My guess is that you already have, especially in the car to and from Mass. Trying again, you could say something like, "Dad is an adult, and he makes his own decisions. I can't tell Dad what to do about church. You are my son. I am responsible before God to raise you as well as I can. And that means teaching you about Jesus and his Church. When you are an adult, you will make your own decisions. Right now, I must decide what is good for you."

Now I ask you, with such loving, irresistible reasoning, how you could not hear, "Gosh, Mom, I've never looked at it that way before. You are so heavenly connected. That's why you're my teacher, and I'm your disciple. What time is Mass again?"

If your son's main motive is "I don't want to," you won't completely lay to rest his "Why doesn't Dad?" however flawless your logic. Nonetheless, you have stated your position clearly. Sometimes that's the best a parent can do.

Next, explain your son to your husband. Tell him that your son is citing him as his reason for resisting Mass. A parent at ease with his own church absence may not be so with his child's. While he personally opts out of Mass, he may not want his child to. If this is your husband's attitude, it introduces a couple of positive possibilities.

One, your husband will support you more openly. Two, he slowly will move back to church himself. To paraphrase the prophet Isaiah, a little child will lead him (Isaiah 11:6).

For some years, I taught a Bible study for inmates at a county jail. The guys brought with them a wide mix of upbringing and beliefs. When I'd ask, "Why are you here?" I'd often hear something like, "I wasn't raised in any church, but I had an aunt who was real religious, and every once in a while, she'd take me to church with her." The mustard seeds of belief were scattered young and, though dormant for a time, sprouted in an adult moved to check out this Christian idea.

Your son, as he tries to move into a more masculine adolescence, may not be attracted to his mother's religious bent. With or without Dad's help, however, you are giving him a look at eternity, something that Dad, at this time, has stopped looking toward.

And who knows, your faithfulness may eventually open your husband's eyes. I've seen it happen.

Imperfect Motivation

Dear Dr. Ray,

My husband attends Mass with me and my two sons, but he says he's doing so for me. I want him to go because of his own beliefs.
—*Dispirited*

Catholic theology talks of "imperfect contrition," meaning sorrow for sins motivated mainly by the fear of punishment—more particularly, hell. Sorrow for having offended God is somewhere in the mix, but it is not primary. Although imperfect contrition is not the ideal, it is sufficient to obtain God's mercy. It is a starting point on the way to more perfect contrition, motivated by love of God. With time and grace, a self-oriented motive can progress into a God-oriented one.

In marriage counseling, a wife might express her wish that her husband be more affectionate. He responds that, by nature, he's not an affectionate guy. Yet for her sake, he'll work on it. In the wife's eyes, this is imperfect affection. That is, Hubby is not being affectionate because he feels it; instead, it's to please her. Still, his motive is honorable. Indeed, a good spouse regularly steps outside of "who they are" and acts to please the other.

Some couples seek counseling when their marriage is barely breathing. One or both would prefer to leave. However, for the sake of the kids, they mutually agree to persevere. In fact, many troubled marriages not only survive but heal because one or both spouses work at it for the kids' sake. For a while, the children are the sole reason Mom and Dad stick together, but that buys time for the reasons to accumulate. When the kids ultimately move on, the parents have a stable relationship.

Psychology 101: The motives underlying a behavior can evolve. A five-year-old doesn't hit his sister because she'll hit him back or because he'll be punished. A ten-year-old doesn't hit his sister because he knows it's wrong. A fifteen-year-old doesn't hit her because she has cute girlfriends. OK, sometimes motives do regress temporarily on one's way to maturity.

Understandably, you want your husband to attend Mass because he loves God. That's the purest motive. Perhaps that motive is acting in some measure, however small, or he wouldn't accompany you at all. He'd feel the hypocrite. For now, accept the fact that your spouse is at Mass for you and with you. And whether or not he realizes it, he is placing himself in God's presence. Take consolation that a God-seeking seed may be present and could grow.

What if he begins to lose his interest in accompanying you? Don't pressure. Allow him to retreat and restart when he wishes. If he's going to Mass for you, you want him to do it willingly.

Part-Time Religion

Dear Dr. Ray,

My wife divorced me three years ago. We have shared custody of our twelve-year-old son and nine-year-old daughter. Their mother practices little religion. I take the children to church when they are with me, but I worry that their exposure to the faith is not consistent enough.

—*Weekend Dad*

Bad news and good news. First the bad news: Your influence is less now than when you and their mother were together, even if you didn't share a family faith. A spouse who is present full-time, even in a troubled marriage, almost always has more influence than one who is present part-time after divorce. That is a hard and sad outcome of a family breakup. Both parents have less parental power. What their kids see, hear, and do in the other house is beyond their reach for the most part. And if one spouse or both remarry, the addition of another parent or two dramatically complicates the dynamics.

Now some good news. As a single parent, you still can show your kids a Christian worldview. You, the parent who takes the faith seriously, must give your children what you can when you can.

That parent being the father brings added hope. One survey found that when both parents attend church with the children, 60 to 80 percent of the children are likely to attend church as adults. If only Dad attends with them, the likelihood remains close to the same. Exactly why isn't clear, but this fact does underscore a father's power as a spiritual model.

The saying is, Mothers make boys; fathers make men. Your son is watching you. If he sees his father living his faith both inside and outside the church doors, those doors will open wider for him. Dad doesn't only trudge him to Mass on Sunday, he prays by his and his sister's bedsides. Dad reads the Bible in full view of his children. Dad leads mealtime blessings, in restaurants even. Dad doesn't disparage Mom for her lack of religion. In all, Dad is a better father because he is a man of God.

A little girl looks at Daddy through a softer lens. His religious ways make him a warmer person. She can count on him to be there for her. He is her defender, her hero. Never underestimate the appeal of a hero image, particularly one shaped by God's hand. Your faith will speak much more clearly to your daughter as she feels its expression throughout her childhood.

What does their mother think of your convictions? Does she respect your right to teach the children when they are with you? Obviously, this would make your life easier. Or does her disagreement extend to disdain? Does she actively undercut not only your religion but your parenting? No doubt this would complicate your fatherhood, especially as the children get older and have their own faith questions.

No matter their mother's attitude, you are still the main, perhaps the only, Bible and Church your children see right now. You are giving them the truth of life, which they may not get anywhere else.

Whether or not your children will embrace the Church as young adults, you can't know. You couldn't know for sure had you and their mother remained one in marriage. What you can know for sure is that you are using your time now to be a faithful father. You are showing them that their dad isn't just a religious guy; he also loves them, supports them, and sacrifices for them. And that is your most durable witness.

Attention Deficit

Mass, the very summit of Catholic worship, deserves the spiritual best of all graced to be present. So why is it so hard for us to stay present there?

From our young ones, controlled disruption is routinely the best we can expect. As kids age, they no longer submarine beneath the pews or wail at ninety-two decibels. Mostly they stay still and silent, sometimes too much so.

We longtime Mass goers can give the impression that we're one with what's before us. Yet our minds can be off somewhere, sometimes far from the sanctuary.

Fortunately, there are ways to keep the little ones physically aimed toward the altar and us bigger ones spiritually aimed toward God.

Mass Maneuvers

Dear Dr. Ray,

How can I get my fourteen-month-old to behave at Mass?
—*Crying Mom*

Can you ask an easier question? Such as, "How can I get the earth to spin in the reverse direction?" Or, "How can I build a cold fusion nuclear reactor in my backyard?" Or, "How can I get my husband to pick up his dirty socks?"

Allow me to answer your question with *my* questions. (We shrink types do that when we have no ready answer.)

What makes you think you can participate peacefully in anything with a fourteen-month-old, for a full hour no less?

What exactly do you mean by "behave"? No whining? No audible fussing? No playing "Look how cute I am" during the homily with the two retirees one row back? How about we think of behaving as minimal disruption? A savvy parent sometimes has to relax her definitions.

Toddlers are old enough to create relentless turbulence but not quite old enough to learn from discipline, which only makes them louder. Give me a sixteen-year-old over a sixteen-month-old, in public anyway.

Celebrating—maybe the operative word is *maneuvering*—Mass with a toddler is a little like street police work. Spells of relative calm are unpredictably shattered by chaos. Your goal is not to make it without incident to the "Go in peace." It is to increase the peace between incidents, looking to the day your child will reverently absorb the celebration—somewhere around age twenty. Just kidding—sort of.

At fifty-nine, try as I might, I seldom reach 100 percent presence at Mass. Something or someone always distracts me. Usually it's somebody's kid.

To prolong the calm—you're not going to get attention at four-teen months—bring along some toddler tranquilizers: a cloth book or two (paper rustles and melts in the mouth); something to suck on, chew on, or drink from—a pacifier (now there's a misnomer), bottle, Sippy cup, his toes; a soft toy, stuffed animal, or favorite blanket. Leave at home anything that uses batteries or makes a sound when dropped from nine inches or less. His shoes?

Travel light. Don't haul in half the child's bedroom, Grandma's Christmas Toys "R" Us warehouse, and the Bible Buffet. More stuff only supplies more material for disruption. Follow the airlines' rule: Try to get everything in one small carry-on.

What about sitting in the front so little John Paul can be mesmerized by the priest's movements? That's one option. But can you actually make it to Mass early enough to snag the front pew? Little kids move in a time warp. You may have to sleep on the church steps the previous night.

If you don't occupy the very front, your child will mostly see backsides, unless you hold him for one hour. Even with that, all the distracting faces sit behind.

Better to plant yourself toward the back. If your child acts up and you can't soothe or distract him, the farther back you're seated, the better. It's a long mile from the front pew to the vesti-bule. Dozens of eyes will follow you and your crabby kid, with thoughts like, "Why didn't she just sit in the cry room in the first place?" or, "Mine knew better than to act like that." Walking a tightrope across Niagara Falls carrying a cougar would seem the shorter trek.

Borrowing the master's words in the wedding parable, "Give place to this man" (the one with the well-behaved kids), and "take the lowest place" (Luke 14:9). From the rear pews, sanc-tuary is only a few short feet away. But don't let John Paul roam around the foyer. He's to be in your arms—with no books, toys, computer, cell phone, or big wheel. Show him that it's better to be back inside.

If your thinking is to immerse John Paul in the Mass at a young age, you may be a shade early, developmentally speaking. Not until age three or so will much register in his memory. Your immediate goal, wherever you sit, is to immerse him in pleasant preoccupations. And if the Mass breaks in here and there, count your blessings.

So, did I answer your question? I did and I didn't. No, there are no strategies this side of heaven to guarantee hour-long toddler cooperation, except sleep—his, not yours. Yes, there are strategies to keep you both inside semi-peacefully for longer periods—your aim for this Church calendar year.

I think I read somewhere that the world record for a parent and toddler coming and going during one Mass is seventeen times. In defense of the parent, it was an Easter Vigil, with all the readings and eleven baptisms.

The Good Young Days

Dear Dr. Ray,
As a toddler, my son was much better behaved in Mass than he is now at age three.
—*No Sign of Peace*

Managing a one-year-old involves three S's—Supervise, Sidetrack, and Stop. Managing a two-year-old adds a fourth S: standard discipline—expectations backed by consequences. It's an addition helpful to both parent and child.

Near age twenty months, our oldest son, Andrew, began to consider himself a bit too grown-up for his little-kid bedtime. One evening, at peak bedtime bad time, I hustled him to the corner for the very first time in his life. Watching, my wife chided me. When I defended myself with, "He needed to be put there," she replied, "I know, but I wanted to be the first one to do it."

Apparently, following ten feet behind Andrew all day every day while I was safely ensconced somewhere writing parenting books had primed her to anticipate the day, or night, she could put more discipline oomph to her words. She had earned the privilege.

Your son is more willful now than he was two years ago. That's pretty typical. And you have more discipline flexibility now than you did two years ago. That's pretty fortunate.

Begin with a few leftover toddler tactics. Let Pius keep company with a small picture book, stuffed animal, or toy. These don't compete with the Mass. They settle little children. And settled is a forerunner to well behaved.

Be satisfied with forward orientation: Allow Pius some latitude in where he looks, sits, stands, or even sleeps, as long as most of the time he's oriented toward the front of the church. No climbing over, under, around, or through the pew. No playing hide-and-seek with the five-year-old three seats back. Proper body disposition precedes proper behavior disposition, with little kids anyway.

A few older folks—those who brought young kids to Mass forty-five years ago—might think Pius is cute. But "cute" fades fast with obnoxious repetition. Head to the vestibule at the first squeak of trouble. Don't wait for the commotion to get loud enough to drown out the priest. This is not admitting defeat or rewarding Pius with a get-out-of-Mass-free card. This is prudent parenting, and it protects those around you from a near occasion of sin.

Seek a sanctuary (not *the* sanctuary) for discipline. The vestibule probably has a bathroom, and bathrooms have corners. Your car comes standard with a car seat; ignore Pius from the front seat until he calms down.

Heading to Grandma's after Mass? Her place should have lots of corners, though Grandma might decry their being so misused on her misunderstood grandson. (Are these the same people who raised us?)

Home will dramatically expand your discipline options. But would you be waiting too long? Shouldn't disciplining young children follow closely after the misbehavior?

Mostly that's so with children younger than your son. At three and a half, he's quite capable of linking what he did then to what you're doing now, especially if you remind him, "Pius, you didn't listen to Mommy at church. Now you have to put your head down at the table."

For multiple disruptions, try multiple consequences. "No cookie today, because you ate a page out of the missalette. Your bedtime doggie is on the refrigerator, because you stepped on your sister's head to climb over the seat. And you're not getting a red

Corvette at your high school graduation; we had to leave Mass three times."

Voice your expectations before Mass. "Pius, if you bang the kneeler up and down, when we get home, you'll go to your bedroom." Is this planting ideas into his liturgical repertoire? Your son doesn't need your ideas. He has more than enough of his own.

Would too much post-Mass discipline sour Pius on the Mass? Does it follow that any discipline anywhere risks a psychological backlash? If you discipline Pius at Grandma's, will he avoid Grandma? If you require a bedtime, will he hate his bed, bedroom, and sunset? All discipline takes place somewhere about something, typically many times. Such is the reality of childhood, indeed adulthood.

Pius may be rowdy, but he's not dumb. He shouldn't need too many weeks to learn better behavior or, at the least, to fall asleep faster. Teaching him the beauty of the Mass begins with not permitting him to be ugly during it.

I'm Conscious

Dear Dr. Ray,

My sixteen-year-old son seems oblivious during Mass. He doesn't sing, seldom responds, and does more staring off than anything else.

—Watching

It's an irony of age. Little kids get manic at Mass; big kids get comatose. Little kids are in perpetual motion; big kids go through the motions. The transformation evolves subtly over a decade or so. Whatever happened to the seven-year-old who used to play Mass in the living room?

What accounts for this all too common teen picture? Does it have something to do with the nature of adolescence itself—that is, an apathy toward the things of grown-ups, a.k.a. old people? Is it a stage, something that will subside with time? Is it rebellion? My parents want me here more than I do, so I'll be here—kind of.

Likely, a piece of all these is present. Still, even taken together, they don't fully explain this mass Mass apathy. For that, another uniquely modern force must be recognized, one fueled by adrenaline. The typical teen's lifestyle is a string of go-go, get-get, do-do stimulation, crammed with technology, rushing images, and entertainment. By comparison, the Mass is prayerful, thoughtful, and beautifully similar across time and place. As it is meant to be.

The contrast is marked. Compared to what kids see and live the rest of the week, the Mass looks and sounds out of phase. Where are the graphics and special effects? Who wrote this script? Much of it is the same as last week's. Reverence is perceived as slow motion, the uniformity as routine. Thus, not only kids but many adults labor to slow down and contemplate. The measured pace is not one that characterizes many of their other pursuits.

Thanks be to God, some of the craving for an ongoing emotional rush eases with age or with having children of one's own. Prayerfully contemplating the liturgy comes more naturally. Meanwhile, what can you do about your son's worship style?

Keep perspective. The average teen is not in the same spiritual place as his religious parent or parents. Maturing in the faith, like any kind of maturing, is typically a process that takes many years and is marked by slips and slides along the way. How much time and grace did you need to better appreciate the holy? How much time and grace do you still need? Keeping this perspective will calm some of your anxiety over your son's present spiritual bent.

Also, most Mass-going teens believe in God, Christ, and his Church. Their disinterest doesn't necessarily signal a creeping apostasy (or disbelief, for those of you who didn't pay attention in catechism class). It reflects more of an attitude that says, "I'm not getting much out of church right now, so I'm not putting much into it." Of course, the truth is that you get back what you first put in.

Apathy borders on disrespect, if it does not equal it. Lack of response reflects lack of respect. Tell your son you expect him to be respectful of God and his house, no matter how he feels about it and no matter whether he wants to or not. He doesn't have to belt out hymns, but he does have to pray with the Mass. Speaking the words is a first step to involvement. The heart may follow in time.

With only twelve years between the oldest and youngest of my ten children, my wife and I have sat at Mass with three to six teens. The passivity that you see I too have witnessed up close and personal. Some of our kids needed only a few lectures about showing respect to engage better. And others answered me with the same glazed look they wore inside the sanctuary.

When mere words didn't elicit cooperation—alas, a standard case with offspring—I set a rule: "Ignore God in his house, and if we go out for breakfast, you watch." For a few weeks my breakfast bill was pretty light. After that, even the holdouts started to get the idea. Food: a prime mover of the soul. (If we planned to go straight home, I had a whole range of other consequences.)

Am I saying you should discipline for disinterest? Your call. There is nothing psychologically incorrect about curtailing a few perks—if merely post-Mass donuts—because of deliberate indifference. The principle is one of respect. What would you do if your son were rude to you? Are you more deserving of respect than the Father?

Here, There, and Everywhere

Dear Dr. Ray,
How can I expect my children to be reverent at Mass when I can't stay focused myself?
—The Drifter

How can your kids tell you're not focused? You're not playing peek-a-boo with the lady behind you, are you? Are you counting how many people are wearing shorts? The number of ceiling-fan rotations per minute? Most likely your drift is internal. Your mind may be meandering, but your body is stationary.

Fortunately, your roving thoughts are not all that noticeable to your kids. If they were, you'd hear about it. Besides, your kids are probably not even looking at you. Others are more interesting. "How did that lady's hair get to be that color?"

If you can, do what savvy parents do: Fake it. Your children don't know when your head is elsewhere, so look present. Fold your hands. Kneel straight up; don't rest your bottom on the pew. Practice reverence, and reverence will become your practice.

You and I share the same mental struggle. I begin Mass with an earnest resolve. I'm there to worship, pray, respond, commune. And I do well, for about the first six minutes. Then I notice a flaw in the wall behind the priest. And my thoughts head to the races: "I never saw that crack before. It wouldn't take much to patch and repaint. I patched a bigger one in the garage last week, and you can hardly tell. But it still needs to be painted. I think I've got some touch-up paint in the basement. I can get to it Saturday before we head up to the game. It's a big one. They're fighting for first place."

In seconds I go from a wall blemish to a pennant race. Other free associations can flow at any time during Mass.

So how do you—and I—stay connected at Mass? The first step involves the eyes—specifically, their movement. Resist canvassing the congregation (Who is that woman with him?) or trying to pinpoint which kid is causing all the commotion (Why doesn't she deal with her?). In short, narrow your field of vision. Keep it directed toward the altar area.

The second step also involves the eyes. Close them, not during the whole Mass but selectively: during prayers, the Consecration, even the readings. Most sensory input comes through the eyes. Thus, most distractions come through the eyes. Closed eyes suppress distractions.

At the least, you'll look holier. Can you levitate? Make sure to open your eyes before you try.

The other senses aren't so readily misdirected. I can't recall too many times when my nose distracted me, except maybe when the kids were real little.

Third step: Orient your ears. Therapists practice something called "active listening." It means to pay close attention to what another is actually saying, in order to grasp its real meaning. Actively listen during Mass. What are the words communicating?

Recent changes in some Mass prayers have told me that my listening is often passive, not active, and my responses rote. For example, for nearly five decades, when the priest prayed, "The Lord be with you," I returned, "And also with you." The response is now the more traditional "And with your spirit." Many Masses passed before I finally answered correctly every time. Most humbling was hearing my wife giggle whenever I caught myself and clumsily corrected with something like, "And also with you... your Spirit."

As any good counselor will tell you, good listening does not come easy or natural. It takes conscious effort. The Prayer after

Communion is a brief, fervent request for the Lord's help to live in thanksgiving for what we've just received. Only when I will myself to listen closely do I hear the prayer's intent.

The temptation is to label attention drift as spiritual weakness. Not necessarily so. Our innate tendency is toward waning attention, especially with something comfortable and familiar, as is the Mass. Someone somewhere once said that good worship does not lie solely in the act of worship but also in the act of pulling oneself back to worshiping.

One last point: You don't have to be the perfect model for everything you teach your kids. If that were so, you'd have little right to teach them much of anything. Human frailty and sin constantly conspire to keep us from the standards we espouse.

The fact that you're not yet the example you want to be—and never will be on this side of eternity—in no way lessens your moral authority. Most of us want our kids to stand morally taller than we do. We don't want to be the upper limit of what they can become.

Drifting focus is unintentional—most of the time anyway. Regaining focus is intentional. Thus, a conscious move toward the Mass is praiseworthy more than an unconscious move away from it is blameworthy.

Do you hear what I'm saying?

Section Three

New Person, Old Past

Coming to Christ for the first time, or growing closer to him with time, Scripture tells us, creates a new person; the old fades (see 2 Corinthians 5:17). Living as a new person will slowly erase the reverberations of one's previous life. But sometimes, direct damage control is necessary. There can be fallout from our past that needs to be repaired.

Even so, it is better to be a new person in faith, conscious of one's struggles and regrets, than to stay the old person, oblivious to what truly matters.

The Way We Were

Dear Dr. Ray,
Throughout my late teens and twenties, I lived a far-from-moral life. My faith reawakened shortly after the birth of our first child. My three children, all teens now, know a little about my past but none of its ugly details. How much, if anything, do I tell them?
—*Private?*

None of it. End of answer. This book has an editor, however, who says I have to say more. Use some questions to guide your decision. Why now? Why to them? What good will it do?

Why now? Is the reason chronological? Meaning, should your kids know more because they're older? Do you know people older than your kids? Have you told them?

My guess is that your parents are older than both you and your kids. Do they know *all* of what you did? Half of it? OK, 16 percent of it? Do you want to fill them in? You'll probably only make them feel inept as parents or clueless. Save their dignity. Age is not a good rationale for telling someone something he has no need to know.

Complete openness in any relationship is seldom wise. In a spasm of brutal self-disclosure, try telling a relative or friend, "I've never really liked you, and I doubt that you will ever be easy to get along with." Open, honest, not smart. Some remarks are better left unsaid, and some mistakes are better left buried in the past.

Sometimes a relative, often a grandparent, unthinkingly or deliberately pushes you to disclose things. She might say to you, within earshot of the kids, "It amazes me that you turned out as good as you did. I was worried there for a while." Or, "I don't know why you're so hard on them, especially the way you were at that age." Or she tells your children, "Hey, kids, you ought to ask your dad sometime about his young escapades."

Even when relatives don't enlighten them, as kids get older, they become more savvy social mathematicians. They add up the bits—comments, old photos, jokes, faded tattoos?—and begin to suspect that their now morally stable parent was once morally wobbly.

You can also create your own pressure to be open. Out of left-over guilt or the belief that total honesty is part of a healthy transparency, you can feel, as the shrinks would say, "a need to share." Don't do it. (Another of my pithy pieces of guidance.)

No matter who is applying pressure, it's you who decides how much to explain your youth. My suggestion: Speak in generalities; avoid specifics. Reveal lessons learned, but skimp on the who, what, when, where, and how. Acknowledge your old self, but don't make it an afternoon TV talk show.

"Yes, I did things I shouldn't have and wish now I hadn't. For sure, I was younger and dumber. My past is partly why I'm the parent I am today with you kids."

Next question: Why to them? Is there something special about being your offspring that entitles them to your past? Because they're close blood relatives? The fact is that those closest to us often need the most protection from our poorer conduct—present or past.

Are you afraid they'll find out about you someday—where's Grandma?—and you'll have to put all the gory details in context? If so, do your damage control then. No need to anticipate what ifs? and answer them before they happen. A line from Colonel Nathan Jessup in *A Few Good Men*: "You have the luxury of not knowing what I know." Let your kids live in luxury.

The most pressing question: What good will it do? It's one to ask yourself any time an unspoken, hard truth is about to be spoken. How will your kids benefit from knowing just how bad you were? Will they relate to you better? "Gee, Mom (Dad), you were once a lot worse than I am now. We have more in common than I thought. I feel the connection, don't you?"

Or will it give your children a ready rationale for their misconduct? "You did more as a teenager than I'm doing. See, this stuff is normal."

Will telling your children about your past raise or lower your moral authority? Will you hear, "I never realized how much you've changed from the way you were, Father. You have so much to teach me"? Or will you hear, "How can you tell me what's right or wrong when you lived the way you did? It was all right for you, but it's not all right for me?"

Whenever a parent watches his kids drift toward his old morals, he may feel the urge to drive them back toward his present morals by sharing his past. More often than not, that doesn't work so well. Kids are prone to interpret such information as grounds for their own misconduct. If someone young or old really wants to do something, he searches hard for a justification. You don't want to be that justification.

So what, if anything, do you tell? Once more, be general. Focus on why you now are who you are as a parent. Your rules and supervision have roots in your personal experience. You know firsthand what can happen when a child maneuvers around a parent's guidance. In short, your past helped shape your present.

Most kids are not of the age or maturity to benefit from their parents' misspent youth. There are better ways for them to learn.

So Did You

Dear Dr. Ray,
How do I respond to an adolescent boy who, upon having social limits put on him, accuses, "You did worse when you were my age."
—*Dumber Then*

Well, did you? If so, whatever he knows about it, don't give him more grist. (See previous question and response.) Your past, however wrong or stupid, is not his concern unless you wish it to be. Remember though, what you say can and will be held against you.

Now let's answer your son. First and foremost, your moral authority as a parent does not depend one whit upon your moral conduct as a teen. The very process of maturing implies that we are more foolish and shortsighted when younger. However you wish to impart this truth to your son, do so. Don't expect him to understand or agree. That's part of his immaturity. Nevertheless, by making your case, you are in essence saying, "Childhood illogic will not weaken my resolve as a parent or cripple me with guilt."

Next, admit to your son an inarguable reality: You were once a child. "You're right, I did teenager things when I was a teenager." Again though, you don't have to reveal all or feel obliged to respond to each of his probing questions. I suspect he's not so much interested in your youth as in getting ammunition for his.

Point three: Contrary to what your son thinks, you are not so old as to recall only in a misty haze what impulses, desires, and dangers accompany youth. It is your memory of once living at his age that makes you acutely aware of your duty to help him safely travel similar roads. Part of being a good parent is remembering being bad as a kid.

Now your masterstroke. Tell your son he is very lucky that you once did wrong and bad things—though you certainly don't do them anymore. Through your firsthand, personal experience with wrong behavior, you realize how critical it is to protect him from his own potential mistakes. Whatever you might have once gotten away with was not to your benefit.

Relevant here is an adage I once heard: A foolish person doesn't learn from his mistakes; a smart person learns from his mistakes; a really smart person learns from the mistakes of others.

You could say to your son, "You're right. I did do worse than you when I was your age. And now I want to raise a kid who's a lot better than I was. And I think that's happening."

This might really irk your son. Not much bugs a teen more than a parent who compliments at the same time she disciplines.

Conversion Guilt

Dear Dr. Ray,
I returned to the Church two years ago, at age forty-three. Until then, I raised my children (now ages sixteen and twelve) with Christmas-and-Easter religion. I've got lots of guilt over the lost years. And my kids have been slow to accept a deeper faith for themselves.
—Too-Late-Smart Mom

Thanks be to God, he opened your eyes. While his presence has transformed your life later than you'd like, it is not too late. A late conversion is infinitely better than no conversion.

Of course, had you stayed as you were in the past, you wouldn't be nagged by present regrets. You might have been able to ignore the God-sized holes in your and your children's lives, for a while anyway. But awareness is almost always a better state than ignorance. It is generally better to feel bad over what was missed than to never know what was missed.

Does this mean you should live with guilt as the natural byproduct of lost opportunity? Not at all. It means, live grateful for where you are now, though you would change the past if you could. Gratitude will trump guilt. It's hard to feel guilty when you're grateful. And you now have something infinitely valuable to share with your children.

Guilt is stoked by self-blame: Why didn't I see the light sooner? Why did I chase the wrong things? Why should my children have to suffer for my blindness? How could I fail in my most important responsibility? Is it too late?

Let's answer emotion with reason. Not all who come to Christ come young, as babies or children. Some of the holiest saints found God in adulthood. All the apostles were called as grown-ups.

God's plans are a mystery. But be assured that he must want you where you are now. Will you question his timing?

Conversion brings forgiveness. God pardons what you did or didn't do as a mom. Though you were directed by your rules, not God's, you didn't fully realize that. You loved your children as you thought best, though your thinking wasn't complete. God is not holding your "failures" against you. Will you argue with his mercy? Will you debate God's wisdom?

A priest told me that moving closer to Christ is like moving closer to a very bright light. As we near, we notice flaws in ourselves that we never saw before. In your young motherhood, you were satisfied with your own self-generated light. Then you came face-to-face with the real Light. Now, not only can you see more clearly where to walk, but that light also shines on anyone you are holding by the hand.

Your kids may want their old mom back. She gave them more freedoms. She thought more as their friends' parents do; she followed cultural trends. This new mom is making some course changes. She's raising her moral bar, tightening some rules. Who is this woman, anyway? Who has taken over her body? Indeed, who?

Their objections aside, the kids can't help but notice that this new mom is a better person. She's more caring, affectionate, and giving. Her discipline is softer, with less scolding and volume. The kids feel positives coming with the negatives. As they mature, they'll feel the positives even more durably.

You say that your children have been slow to accept a deeper faith. That's not unexpected. You willingly chose to change; they may not be quite there yet. Don't let guilt push you to preachy pushiness. Be patient.

Patience, however, doesn't equal the attitude that allows you to say, "This is their decision. I won't try to influence them." Certainly do try to influence them. Act on the faith: Attend Mass together (that's nonnegotiable), take turns praying before meals, bless them at bedtime, read the Bible, sign them up for CCD, find charitable activities for your family to be involved in, and educate on morals and virtue. Show them that what you found you want to give.

A final piece of good news: While your children don't see this through forty-three-year-old eyes, they've gotten an earlier start than you. Total their ages, and you get twenty-eight, still fifteen years shy of your age at rebirth.

New Old Wife

Dear Dr. Ray,

My husband and I have been married thirteen years—no children. For most of that time, we were both non-practicing Catholics. In the last three years, I've had a strong awakening of my faith, and my husband is not so happy with the new me. He says I'm not the same woman he married.

—Remade

He is right. You are not the same woman he married. Indeed, are you a better one?

It is the rule rather than the exception: No two spouses are on the exact same spiritual page. Some aren't even in the same book. While one has memorized the daily Mass times at all parishes within a twenty-five-mile radius, the other struggles to stay awake during a six-minute Sunday homily. One prays the rosary in Aramaic while levitating; the other needs a teleprompter to say a complete Glory Be.

Sometimes the roles shift. Having been raised solidly Catholic, I took the lead Church-wise upon meeting my wife, Randi, who grew up with little formal religion. In a word, I appeared the more "religious" one. A few years into our marriage, Randi turned more strongly to Christianity and ultimately to Catholicism. I'd like to believe my holy example influenced her, but she maintains that were it not for me, she would have converted sooner.

My wife's conversion was at once fervent and continues to be so. It's now plain to anyone paying attention that she is the more religious one. Though in my defense, I no longer need a teleprompter, even for the Apostles' Creed.

Whatever the spiritual distance between you and your husband, don't let it be a source of strife. Without weakening your internal

God presence, you can modify your external expression of it.

For instance, if you attend weekday Mass, don't always attend when Hubby is home. Work your Mass schedule around his work schedule and his other times out of the house. Arrange church activities that compete least with marriage activities. Don't fill most of your free time with parish functions, including protracted phone calls with new, like-minded church friends.

Preset one, not every, Christian station on your car radio. When driving together, listen to what your husband prefers. I know, you could care less about the ongoing debate over the benefits of the designated hitter in baseball. But for now, this may be where his mind plays.

Is your husband bothered by your fading interest in his, and once your, favorite TV programs? Without relaxing your morals, find things to watch together—football, World War II chronicles, *Modern Tank Repair*, *Gator Guys*—the stuff wives record to watch again and again.

Our Lord teaches, "But when you pray, go into your room and shut the door and pray to your Father who is in secret" (Matthew 6:6). Lower the profile of your prayer time and spiritual reading. And for sure, don't speak to your husband in Latin.

Your spouse may not so much be threatened by your new life; he may believe that your old life with him is passing. As he feels left out of your world, he may resent your world. Find more ways to enter his. Read up on the designated hitter pros and cons. Ask him if it's smart to call a draw play on third down and twelve.

None of this is to deny Christ or his Church. Nor is it to hide your light under a basket. Your husband knows who you are and what you treasure. You are not weakening your connection to God; you are strengthening your connection with your spouse.

Now for your best option. It's hard, but it has the most potential to draw your husband closer to you and to the faith. Show him how much the new you benefits him. Show him that his post-conversion wife is a better spouse than his pre-conversion one—more agreeable, more giving, more affectionate, overall just sweeter to live with. I know, it's a whole lot easier to pray alone in the car than to improve one's personality. Changing oneself, however, is the best way to change another.

Are you already the much sweeter spouse? If so, are you at your holiness limit? Did you rise there in just three years? That's fast. The paradox of faithful living: The more you mature, the more you have room to mature.

What if your husband takes advantage of his ever more saintly wife? She is more compromising, so he becomes less compromising. She is more pleasant, so he is less pleasant. This is unlikely. Most people react positively to better treatment; very few react negatively. Your spouse may not be all that religious, but he's probably not all that unreasonable. When someone's behavior makes another's life better, the other person almost always welcomes it.

How long until your noticeably more loving wifehood noticeably converts your husband's attitude? I have no idea. (Did you spend your own money on this book?) But I do know that however long it takes, you will be moving in a better direction than currently.

Through it all, your motive to be a better spouse is stronger than his. Your faith tells you to be.

New But Not Improved

Dear Dr. Ray,
The more I try to live my faith, the less I like who I am. I think I had a better self-image pre-Christian.
—*Self-Critical*

It may seem so. But upon whose judgment was your self-image based? Yours or God's?

Thinking well of oneself is psychologically pretty easy: Avoid honest self-scrutiny. At the least, don't look too far inward for the stuff of human frailty.

Once upon a time, you were your own judge of your virtue. You set the standards, so how could you not be satisfied with you? A natural human inclination is to lower one's personal moral bar to meet one's overall conduct. It's a defense in service of the ego.

Because you now desire to live more for God and less for yourself, it's understandable to experience some frustration. The more you look inside, the more you realize where and how you're not following Christ on the outside. From the seemingly slow pace of your spiritual growth springs the self-critique.

One other fellow talked of this same frustration long ago. His name was Paul. "I do not understand my own actions. For I do not do what I want, but I do the very thing I hate" (Romans 7:15).

Your internal struggle can create what psychologists call "cognitive dissonance." It is the holding of two contradictory ideas in one's head at the same time. One idea is that you believe you can rest in the peace Christ promises his followers. The other is that you feel less than peaceful about your efforts to live for him.

To increase your peace, think less as you and more as Christ. Meaning, keep his promises uppermost in your mind. Remember that his love is unconditional. It doesn't ebb and flow with your moral successes and failures. God values you highly, and he knows your frailty far better than you know it.

Then too, God asks for your effort. To paraphrase C.S. Lewis: God wants people of a certain kind.[1] That is, he doesn't scrutinize our ledger of goods and bads and then decide whether or not he likes us. He wants people who relentlessly seek him, despite their fallen nature. Indeed, the most reliable sign of our love for God lies in our perseverance past our moral stumbles and fumbles. And he gives us the grace to persevere.

Suppose, though, that you start to feel pretty good about your faithfulness. If you have to say so yourself, you're getting to be a pretty holy human. Could this kind of spiritual self-esteem evolve into spiritual pride? Perhaps.

Certainly, one wants to take pleasure in faithful obedience. Just as certainly, one doesn't want to get too self-satisfied. In that direction lurks pride, and pride is a falsely inflated self-image.

Your current low self-image may be feelings fueled by doubt. You don't *feel* good about your faith walk. Because of your moral ups and downs, you *feel* inadequate. Because of your failures, you *feel* unworthy. As I mention elsewhere in this book, feelings are a fickle guide to truth. Because you feel something doesn't make it so. Good thinking has to overrule undeserved bad feelings.

Good thinking begins with accepting reality. And the reality is that you are a better person now than you were pre-Christian. You are living by higher standards. You are more self-aware. And take it from a shrink: It is better to be more self-aware, even if that includes a clear view of one's shortcomings, than to be self-satisfied. Self-satisfaction stunts personal growth. It also keeps one from getting closer to God.

What you are presently is a child of God, one closer to him than you once were. His bright light shows more of your personal flaws, but it also gives warmth and healing. All in all, it's a real good trade-off.

Section Four

Counter Catholic

Bishop Fulton Sheen, a highly respected teacher of the faith in the 1950s and 1960s, once observed, "There are not a hundred people in America who hate the Catholic Church. There are millions of people who hate what they wrongly believe to be the Catholic Church—which is, of course, quite a different thing."[2]

Not to quibble with someone as wise and holy as Bishop Sheen, but I wonder how many people these days denounce the Catholic Church exactly for who she is.

Wrongheaded critiques don't only create religious distance between people. They also create relationship distance. Knowing how and, maybe as importantly, knowing when to answer people who question the faith is a giant step—if not toward full reconciliation, then toward some sense of personal spiritual peace.

Misguided Missionary

Dear Dr. Ray,

My eight-year-old daughter plays with a neighbor girl, age ten. Lately her friend, who is not Catholic, has been talking down our Catholic faith. This is bothering my daughter, but she doesn't want to lose her friend.

—Neighborly Advice?

I've not met one ten-year-old who collects anti-Catholic tracts or who's written a theological treatise on the differing Christian traditions. If by chance she's that one, ask to see her research— prior to the next play date.

If she's a typical ten-year-old, what she is saying is a rephrase of what she is hearing. She is parroting some big people, at home or elsewhere. On her own, she probably hasn't formed too many anti-Catholic sentiments yet.

Since you don't know exactly who is putting these words into her mind, your first step would be toward her house, specifically toward her parents. Describe for them what is happening, using a few concrete examples. Avoid accusations or recriminations. You come in peace. Your mission is a fact-finding one.

Your neighbors may be totally unaware of their daughter's actions. They could be embarrassed. If so, you won't have to say or do much more. They will rein her in. Problem solved. Little friends back to playing together in ecumenical harmony.

On the other hand, they could be pleased that their daughter has learned so young to evangelize. Your approach then becomes more active. Again charitably, tell them you will seek to correct any of their daughter's misunderstandings, for both girls' sake. And if they're open, you'd be willing to clear up any of their own misunderstandings about the Catholic Church.

Their reaction to your offer will speak clearly. Should they accept it, they'll show themselves open to understanding. Should they reject it, and even become upset at your "counter-evangelizing," they may choose to protect their child from you and yours. Much will hinge upon how deep-rooted their misconceptions are.

Defensiveness sometimes subsides when the emotions feeding it do. Perhaps later, your neighbors will settle, rethink the matter, and respect your wishes, allowing the girls to return to uncomplicated friendship. Time and more play visits will tell.

Of course, you may not hear everything from your daughter, as she wishes to protect the friend she wants to keep. Therefore, watch for signs that something is bothering her, especially soon after playing with her friend: a sober mood, vague remarks ("I just wish she'd be nicer"), atypical behavior (retreating to her bedroom), questions such as, "Mom, why do we pray to Mary?" You know your daughter well. You can sense her upset even when she doesn't tell you about it.

Suppose that the juvenile critiques keep coming. If you can use them to educate your daughter, they will strengthen her faith, yours too. If her friend's words are more unsettling to her than your words are comforting, you may have to curtail the friendship or, at a minimum, keep the girls' interactions within your earshot. Your neighbor girl is not a bad influence; her wrongheaded religious prejudices are.

Will your daughter agree with your decision? Probably not. The best of parents are routinely misunderstood—in the short-term, not in the long-term.

Youth Think

Dear Dr. Ray,
My fifteen-year-old daughter has been attending a youth group at her friend's non-Catholic church. It offers social activities and lectures by the pastor. I'm a little nervous about what she could hear about her Catholic faith.
—Wary

I wouldn't at all be nervous, as long as what she's hearing is the truth. Otherwise, I too would be nervous.

Non-Catholic churches have long offered youth groups. Some of these groups are Catholic-charitable, some are Catholic-tolerant, and some are Catholic-hostile. You need to investigate: Which is your daughter attending?

You could ask her what she is hearing there. Her report, however, might not be completely reliable. For one, she may not be aware of whether her Catholic beliefs are being questioned, especially if the questioning is subtle. For another, her enjoyment of the group may slant the picture she presents to you.

You could accompany her a few times. (Gasp! Just walk in twenty minutes apart, sit back by the door, and sport a fake mustache.) Talk with the leaders and pastor. What's their understanding of Catholicism? How do they see it? What do they know? Listen to a selection of the pastor's presentations, in person or recorded. Read the church's mission statement or a sampling of their literature.

Talk to the mother of your daughter's friend or other church members you might know personally. Adult attitudes generally trickle down to the youth. Even if the pastor considers Catholics fellow Christians, some of the congregation might not. Their kids could see it as their Christian duty to pull the new kid out of her "false religion."

Then too, how well does your daughter know her Catholic faith? Can she express it? Defend it? Can she discern a sincere question from a veiled challenge? Or explain a Bible quote that seems to contradict Catholic teaching?

There are teens who are well-spoken missionaries for the Church—for their age. But the most mature teen is still a teen. Faith tempered by fire involves years of experience and truth seeking. Most adolescents are pulled by the social side of youth groups and pay minimal heed to the doctrinal side.

Should all your initial reservations be soothed, remain vigilant. Keep an open dialogue with your daughter. Your aim is to make it easy for her to bring any questions or confusion to you. If some real nonsense surfaces, try to stay calm. The truth has nothing to fear from the false.

Eventually, you may decide you can't completely address or counter the pull of your daughter's friend's religion. Over your daughter's objections, you may have to end her attendance.

The bright side: Good Catholic youth groups are out there. Check with area churches. If you don't find a viable youth group, maybe you can start one!

Higher Reeducation

Dear Dr. Ray,

Our nineteen-year-old son returned home from college this summer full of questions and objections about the Catholic faith. Now he seems to feel obligated to correct his fifteen-year-old brother's thinking.

—In the Middle

The reigning academic mind-set feels obligated to correct, attack even, the thinking of traditionally religious students. Having a child's faith dogmatically assaulted is bad enough; it's even worse to pay someone to do it. Unfortunately, Christian parents in large numbers are unaware of what all is included in a college education these days.

Your son's enlightened thinking is shedding some needed light on your thinking, specifically about his ongoing education. That is, you may have to ask yourself: Is he in the best environment for growth in true wisdom?

It sounds as though your son is bringing his new mind-set home. Before next semester, let's college-proof Younger Brother. First assignment: Rein in Older Brother. Do not permit him to reeducate his sibling.

Invite Older Brother to lay all his newfound knowledge on you or your spouse. Encourage him to tell you exactly what he's being told and by whom. What are the backgrounds and motives of these sources? What is their history? Many objections to religion are based not on reason but on personal emotional experience. Most likely, the arguments that your son finds so intellectually heavy rest on sand. But he doesn't know enough to know that.

As I have emphasized elsewhere, you need to know, or at least find out, how to answer well. If you flounder in the face of your son's queries, you could only convince him that his professors and fellow students are indeed smarter about the real Catholic Church than you are.

The excitement of novel revelations, however wrongheaded, can emotionally drive someone to show another his intellectual superiority. Recognizing this aspect of human nature will dampen your frustration if your son resists bothersome little basics like facts, logic, and reality. He may feel compelled to defend his turf and thus be pushed more by a need to be right than a desire to clear his head. Arrogance often accompanies newly gained knowledge.

What if College Brother continues trying to reeducate Younger Brother? In concluding that he is outgrowing his parent's simplistic thinking, your son may feel a zeal to shape Younger Brother into right thinking. You will then have to act. Consequences will follow: loss of car, computer, cell phone, social freedoms, money. Though he is nineteen, you still have plenty of leverage.

No doubt, your son will believe that you are stifling free speech and academic discourse. So be it. Freedom of speech has its limits. He doesn't need to share his religious reformation with every family member.

Talk too with Little Brother. What has Big Brother told him? What are his questions because of it? What has most bothered him?

Let Little Brother hear the solid answers that the Church has to the antagonistic questions thrown at her. Indeed, the Church has heard it all and has been answering many of the same challenges since the time of Christ. Your son has nothing to fear from the secular dogmas of "really smart" people.

Give your younger son a prerequisite course in religious instruction. In so doing, you'll be preparing him for college.

Bible Versed

Dear Dr. Ray,
I've been attending a women's Bible study at a nondenominational church. I enjoy it and am learning, but some of my Catholic beliefs are being disputed.
—*Lone Voice*

Contrary to popular misunderstanding, the Church has always emphasized knowledge of Scripture. That's why every Sunday Mass has three Bible readings, which cover much of the Old and New Testaments every three years. Formal Bible studies, until relatively recently, have been the mainstay of other Christian groups, as Catholics have traditionally looked toward the Church to teach the faith as well as accurately interpret Scripture. Now Catholic studies are fast on the rise.

Many non-Catholic Bible studies emphasize two basics: One, Jesus is Lord. With that, Catholics fully agree. And two, the Catholic Church is wrong or, worse, evil, as she is leading countless people away from true Christianity.

The Catholic Church is the largest religious body in the United States, with some seventy million baptized. Sadly, those who accept her whole teaching, or even simply attend Sunday Mass, total a much smaller number. It has been said that the second largest religious group in the U.S. consists of fallen-away Catholics, those heading toward either other denominations or a spiritual vacuum.

Predicting by the numbers alone, one or more of your study's members once were Catholic and are carrying with them a raft of misunderstandings or resentments about their former church. Further, their antagonism often is grounded in their personal experience, giving them credibility with the study's non-Catholics.

During my thirties, I drifted from the Church and began to

attend several non-Catholic studies. While I met many sincere, God-seeking Christians, I also met regular anti-Catholic bias—some from ignorance, some from arrogance. In one study, a former Catholic declared with a tone of leftover bitterness, "I was raised Catholic and went to Mass for over twenty years, and I never heard Jesus Christ proclaimed 'Lord and Savior.'"

Out of curiosity, I later obtained a missalette from the previous week's Mass and counted how many times Jesus was called Lord, Savior, Lamb of God, Son of God, God. Total: thirty-six. Note that this did not include any of his titles that the priest used in his homily. I wondered if I should ask my friend, "Where were you all those years?"

At times though, people's arguments did stir up doubts for me. Though I knew the basics of what the Church taught, I didn't know the reasons, from Scripture or history. What if these other Christians were right and the Church was wrong? I mean, they had Bible verses to buttress their case.

Thank God for my growing confusion. It pushed me to seek answers, not from ex- or anti-Catholics but from the Church herself. Obviously, she was no stranger to these objections. Something told me she'd been hearing and dispelling them for centuries—many of them from the time of Christ.

So I read, studied, listened—and found the Church's teachings to make complete sense and to reflect what Christians have historically believed. My search led me back to the Church I knew as a child.

How confident and comfortable are you in answering the misunderstandings you hear? Do you know not only the whats of your faith but the whys? You needn't be a Scripture scholar or theologian before you speak. A well-informed Catholic can well inform anyone open to listening.

The operative adjective is *well-informed*. Trying to muddle one's way through an answer just further convinces people that Catholics don't know much about their faith. As the saying goes, better to stay silent and appear dumb than to open one's mouth and remove all doubt.

As I learned how to better explain Church teaching, some people in my former Bible study were intrigued by what they heard, so much so that they began a personal search and eventually converted. Educate yourself, and then educate others.

And find a good Catholic Bible study. They are out there—more all the time.

Conversion Critiques

Dear Dr. Ray,
My parents raised me in a faithful non-Catholic Christian house-hold. They continue to be upset over my Catholic conversion four years after marrying my Catholic husband. Mostly they avoid the topic, but every so often they demean some Church teaching or practice.
—*Relatively Hurt*

You use the word *demean*. So I'm assuming that the nature or tone of their remarks is hostile toward the Church and hurtful to you. Honest questions deserve honest answers. Critiques often convey that no answers, no matter how gentle and logical, will satisfy.

You must wonder, "Why do they continue to be upset?" Are they taking your conversion personally? That is, not only did you abandon the religion of your youth, but you abandoned the religion they invested so much of themselves in teaching you. In short, you rejected not only their faith but them too.

When time and opportunity permit, address this. Reassure your parents of your gratitude for the foundation they gave you. Let them know that you are now building upon that foundation. Something tells me you've already done this, but I do need to fill out my answer.

Try to persuade your folks—to the degree you can—that your journey to the Catholic Church is not a repudiation of their heart-felt beliefs. Rather your desire is to follow where Christ leads and to worship as a family with your husband (and children).

Ask your parents, "What is a Christian?" Seek their basics for being a follower of Christ. As a Catholic, you will likely be able to agree with most, perhaps all of them. Your message is: I have not left Christianity. I have embraced another expression of it, one that I believe is a fuller one.

Do your mother and father think your husband or his family pressured you to convert? This wasn't your idea, but theirs? What's more, was this persuasion subtle, below your awareness? Be prepared, even as you tell them that wasn't so, to receive a response like, "Well, you may not see it, but in fact…"

You can only articulate your true motives. What they choose to think is beyond your control. Of course, the better you know the faith, the better you can explain your decisions.

When questions, even criticisms, come, it's good to have a restrained, ever-ready reply: "Mom, do you want to know why the Church teaches that?" Or, "I can give you an answer if you want one, Dad." Then listen and observe their demeanor. It should reveal to you, maybe to them, why they are judging as they are. Legitimate misunderstandings can be cleared up with good explanations.

What if your parents aren't the least interested in knowing anything more about the Catholic faith? What if they are convinced of their ideas, not wishing to hear any others?

Do not argue, dispute, or get into a religious tit for tat. That will only increase family tension. To persuade them, you must continue to live by the fourth commandment: Honor thy father and mother. *Honor* does not mean you have to concur with their every thought or obey their every wish. It means you will give them their due respect and act to keep friction to a minimum, especially friction based on religion.

Only as they see that being Catholic is making you a better daughter, wife, and mother will they be inclined to give you and your religion more credibility. Many people are not convinced by arguments, no matter how good. They can, however, be persuaded by good treatment.

Sins against Society

Dear Dr. Ray,
I'm a mother of five children and happily pregnant with my sixth. I'm amazed at how free people feel to disparage my family size. I'm reluctant to tell anyone I'm expecting again.
—*Getting Quieter*

Tolerance is the pervasive, preeminent new moral virtue. Whatever others want to do is their choice, indeed their right, and is to be accepted, even celebrated. Yet our society is quite inflexible about its tolerance. For all its vaunted openness, the tolerance movement is riddled with ironies.

Irony #1: Tolerance is for all, except some. Not everyone deserves to think his or her own way. Tolerance is reserved for those who think the right way, as defined by reigning secular rules. The largest group of "non-acceptables" come from traditional values, especially those of the Christian faith and, most especially, the Catholic faith.

Irony #2: Tolerance redefines itself, moving with cultural winds. One moral edict that nowadays must be accepted is sexual freedom—except, as you hear firsthand, the sexual freedom to have babies in marriage.

Someone once keenly observed, "When people stop believing in God, the danger is not that they believe in nothing, the danger is that they'll believe in anything." In God's absence, or at least his lower profile, society decides to define what constitutes a sin. Three new ones have rapidly emerged: smoking, spanking, and having more than 1.78 children.

Irony #3: Sacrifice is called selfishness. Mothers and fathers who accept children as God's gifts, who daily sacrifice for their larger than standard family, and who live with fewer creature comforts get accused of being selfish or of wanting children in order to meet some underlying psychological needs. It's as if embracing children is a form of greed. Tell that to these parents' checkbooks.

Irony #4: Plenty is no longer enough. No society in human history has enjoyed our level of resources and abundance. Yet a standard objection against having many children is material: How can you take care of them? Meaning what? Food? Shelter? Education? Cars? Bathrooms? Bedrooms?

The typical family home of a generation or two ago was around a thousand square feet. It had one bathroom, two or more kids in a bedroom, no air conditioning, one phone, and a single-car garage. Parents who successfully raised families in such deprived conditions now wonder how their grown children can maintain a favorable family lifestyle in a house twice or more times as large, with multiple everything. One child per bedroom is the acceptable limit.

During my wife's and my adoption screening for our fourth child, the social worker asked us, "Do you have sufficient bedrooms?" I was tempted to answer, "Well, they do have walls, beds, and carpet, but no TVs." But Randi shot me a "don't go there" look. At the time, we had three bedrooms, which seemed quite sufficient to me. As a fallback, Randi and I could move to the couch. Well, maybe I could.

When my oldest daughter, Hannah, entered college, the school's president talked with families about freshman adjustment to having a roommate. At which Hannah exclaimed, "Wow. Only one?" She had entered dormitory heaven.

Irony #5: OK for me, not you. Too-many-kids comments regularly come from those who had large families themselves.

This includes grandparents and others of their generation who routinely had four-plus children. Nevertheless, they now question why their offspring would want more offspring.

Irony #6: People of faith also question. It is understandable that the nonreligious would look askance at parents who challenge the childbearing norm numerically; their perspective is slanted by popular outlook. One would expect people of faith to better understand the God-ordained value of children. Sadly, many observe family life through a lens more secular than faith lit.

Irony #7: One mustn't critique others—except mothers. Those who religiously shun talking politics or religion feel unrestrained license to opine about the most personal of someone's life decisions. The remarks are predictably similar—thought clever but in fact tiresome. "Are they all yours?" "Don't you have a TV?" "So this is it, right?" (This last question usually follows child number two, and it almost always comes after child number three.) "You've got your boy and girl (the complete family), so are you finished?"

Sometimes the intrusions come with an edge: "I hope you're not thinking of more?" "How can you give each the attention it needs?" (The pronoun itself is instructive.) "What about college?" (The financial lurks beneath many comments.)

There is risk to verbally cornering veteran mothers. After all, these are women uncowed by years of living in close proximity to multiple little human beings. A rude remark or two can be swatted away as effortlessly as a seven-year-old's tattle.

"Is this all your family?" "Of course not, our oldest is at home with the triplets."

"Haven't you ever heard of birth control?" "Yes, I've heard of it. Why?"

"Do you know what causes this?" "No, please tell me."
"Is your husband going to get fixed?" "I don't think he's broken."

"Are you going to have more?" "Well, not right this minute."

"Don't you think you have too many children?" "Which one should I give back?"

The most pointed: "I'm glad it's you and not me." "I think my kids are glad too." Ouch!

Sometimes the concerns are for Mom: "I just worry about you." "Be careful you don't overload yourself." "How's your stress level?" "Can you manage it all?" "Are you doing OK?"

Even when well-meaning, these questions imply that Mother doesn't quite understand what she's doing to herself. Isn't she sacrificing herself for all these children? Well, yes, she is. That is exactly her intent.

It's good to answer sour with sweet: "A soft answer turns away wrath" (Proverbs 15:1). "We've always been grateful for our kids." "We want whoever God gives us."

Sometimes a good response is no response—a smile, a shrug, a lost look. Lost looks are good at silently saying, "I don't understand your point." What else can anyone expect from someone who has deliberately fried her brain circuitry with so many children?

In the end, what wins over naysayers most is the children themselves. Parents of plenty typically invest themselves heavily in their families. In time, others will see that your children are not emotionally and materially shortchanged. Rather, they are maturing into individuals to be admired by those who once didn't understand you.

....

Section Five

Faithful Distress

Faith brings beyond-this-world peace. Our Lord is quite clear about that. How, then, can it also bring distress? Simple answer: It can't. It is not the faith that generates inner turmoil; it is misunderstandings about the faith.

If our love for Christ is accompanied by self-reproach, we have to look not at Christ but at ourselves. The question is not "What is it about Christianity that is making me feel bad?" The question is "What am I doing—or what am I thinking—to make me feel bad?"

A Piece of Peace

Dear Dr. Ray,

I know my faith should be a source of peace. But I don't always feel that peace. I worry about sinning, and even after confession, I don't always feel forgiven.

—Praying for Peace

Anytime anyone is passionately moved to do anything well, going to a self-sabotaging extreme is a temptation. Faith is meant to be taken to an extreme—a self-renewing one, not a self-defeating one.

God calls us to have a healthy sensitivity to the sickness of sin. The closer you move toward God, the more you know how ugly sin is. In no way does this awareness mean that you won't sin again, regularly even. It means you don't want to sin. It means your sense of repentance, of wanting to avoid the sin next time, grows stronger. It's been said that the difference between a saint and a sinner is that the saint gets up one more time than he falls.

You say you "worry" about sinning. Someone who seeks sin doesn't worry about it. Worry about sin is one sign that you hate sin. Your lack of peace comes from taking your worry too far.

With the deepest of resolves to shed sin, we still remain at war with our human weakness. And we have some elite company. Read St. Paul's Letter to the Romans, chapter 7: "I do not understand my own actions. For I do not do what I want, but I do the very thing I hate." He laments his condition but rests in the cure: "Thanks be to God through Jesus Christ our Lord" (Romans 7:15, 25).

You have some sentiments in common with Paul—up to a point. He too sees himself as a sinner, but he also trusts in God's pardon.

He sees that he falls because of his human frailty, but he believes that God is ever ready to pick him up.

You use the same word to describe both your lack of peace and your questioning of God's mercy: *feel*. This may reflect the mind-set of our hyper-psychologizing culture. Feelings supposedly reveal the genuine self at the very center of our being. One can't dispute feelings without disputing oneself. Feelings rule.

This view directly clashes with the Christian understanding of humanity. Yes, feelings are an ingrained feature of who we are, but they are subservient to our more God-imaged qualities—intellect and will.

You say you don't *feel* peace or forgiveness. But are your feelings a true reflection of what is? Meaning, are you in fact not in God's peace, and are you in fact not forgiven? Don't let feelings negate God's promises. He promises that an honest confession brings forgiveness—period—independent of what one feels afterward.

Return, O faithless sons,

I will heal your faithlessness. (Jeremiah 3:22)

I can't know exactly what underlies your lack of peace. Guilt over having sinned? Not measuring up to self-imposed saintly standards? Concern that your actions belie your intentions? Not one of these, nor all taken together, trumps God's pledge. Accept him at his word: You are forgiven, no matter what your feelings tell you. What you know must overrule what you feel. Feelings can be the great deceivers.

Christ has said repeatedly—for those of us hard of spiritual hearing—that he wants to forgive. He told Peter that he must forgive "not...seven times, but seventy times seven" (Matthew 18:22). That is biblical language for "completely and continuously." If our Lord wants you to forgive others so fully, does this advice not apply to forgiving yourself? Or to his forgiving you? Does Christ ignore his own teachings?

I previously mentioned something called cognitive dissonance. It comes from holding two opposing thoughts in one's head simultaneously. The clash creates dissonance, a sense of tension or, in your words, a lack of peace. For you, one thought is: I am a Christian, and God loves me. Its antagonist: How can I keep sinning and expect God to keep absolving me?

Simple answer: Because that's who God is. He doesn't have to force himself to be merciful. There is no limit on his occasions of forgiveness (seventy-one times seven?). His being is mercy.

If you willfully, deliberately embrace sin, then a disturbed peace is warranted. Conscience is making its presence felt. If, however, you sin out of human weakness, then whatever guilt remains post-repentance is not from God. It comes out of a misunderstanding of God's ways—or maybe from the devil, "who accuses [us] day and night," even "before our God" (Revelation 12:10).

Peace endures when knowledge and emotions coincide. I feel peace because I know God forgives me. If the head and heart are at odds, however, the head must exert itself. The more it does, the more it will bring wayward feelings into reality.

Peace comes from believing God, not from believing one's feelings.

More Faith, Less Depression?

Dear Dr. Ray,

I'm fifty-three years old and have struggled on and off throughout my life with depression. Since my return to the Church twelve years ago, I've felt that if I had more trust in God, I'd have less depression.

—Better by Now?

Depression has many faces with many causes. Without knowing your personal history, I can't say what underlies your bouts. However, I do know people with similar doubts about their faith.

Some depression is chemical. It is grounded in dysfunctional brain pathways. What these pathways are, medical science is just beginning to unravel. Some depression follows crushing life events—the death of a loved one, a fractured marriage, illness, financial calamity, trauma.

Most depressions are born and raised by how one interprets everyday stresses and strains. Identical circumstances can bury one person in despair and temporarily ruffle another, depending upon the meaning given them.

When the depression is biochemically driven, faith doubts are unfounded. Proper medication—which the Church supports—often raises the mood, which then lowers the self-reproach. With most depression, talk therapy helps, as it aims to uncover and correct whatever "mis-thinking" is fueling the melancholy.

A key piece of your thinking is that your depression is a sign of your weak Christianity. As some psychologists might say, your thought equation is: Less faith equals more depression. There can be some truth to this if questions of religion rattle your moods or if you are scrupulously tormented by thoughts of your sinfulness.

Otherwise, depression typically comes from a mix of causes, with one's faith level a minor factor at most.

If your faith rivals that of God's holiest saints, you can indeed find peace in the middle of emotional upheaval. As St. Paul writes, "For I have learned, in whatever state I am, to be content" (Philippians 4:11). If you're anything like me, however, or pretty much most of Christ's followers, your faith is imperfect: It won't be complete until you see him face-to-face. Until that day, you live in an unfinished state of trust.

Christ puts our faith in perspective, "If you have faith as a grain of mustard seed, you will say to this mountain, 'Move from here to there,' and it will move" (Matthew 17:20). Given that scale, my faith would have to increase many-fold just to reach the size of a mustard seed. This does not mean that more trust in God's providence won't lighten my mood. It will. The error comes in thinking the converse—that is, incomplete faith darkens one's mood.

How can more faith bring more peace? It can change a person's self-view. Depression is routinely wrapped around a poor self-image. "I feel insignificant, worthless even." The experts reiterate that to combat depression, an individual needs to think well of himself, to believe he is a good and worthwhile person. The catch is that the person doing the self-assessment is also the one with the most doubts about his judgment.

If I, Ray Guarendi, declare myself to be a special human being, how much weight does my subjective vote carry? How much credibility do I have to testify to my own specialness? (Though, as a shrink, I suppose I could administer some tests to myself.)

On the other hand, if the Creator of the universe has declared me of infinite worth—as he has—that's indisputable testimony. That's real self-esteem. Accepting God's view of you will dignify your view of you. With that will come more peace.

Depression is also marked by feelings of not being worthy of love. "I don't love me much, and I can't see how others could either." If God, the source of all love, pronounces me lovable—as he does—who am I to question him? Am I more psychologically attuned to me than he is? Trusting God's judgment above my own is a healthy move toward a better mood.

Suppose I grapple with doubts of my competence—as a spouse, a parent, a Christian. Others look so much more capable than I. By comparison, I feel I constantly fall short.

God doesn't grade on a curve. He is not about to fail me because I'm not in the upper 30 percent of child-raising skill, spousal desirability, or Christian saintliness. My achievements or competence have little—sometimes nothing—to do with my connection to God. If God scored us on results, we'd all fall short. I know I'd have to enroll in an ongoing remedial life course.

Indeed, it is often our shortcomings that spur us to reach higher for God. The "people of a certain kind" that God wants are those who continue to seek him no matter what their strengths and weaknesses are.

Faith is an infinite source of emotional strength. With God's help, it will increase until the day we leave this world for the next. In the meantime, to chastise yourself for insufficient faith leading to depression is to misunderstand what faith is. It also shows a misunderstanding of what depression is.

No Time Like the Future

Dear Dr. Ray,

My son is thirty years old. He left the Church shortly after college and has never returned. I've prayed for him so much, but I'm getting discouraged because nothing is changing.
—*Wearying*

Perhaps it should be said this way: Nothing is changing that you can see. Something might well be changing that you can't see. The heart often moves some distance before conduct follows.

Let's talk metaphysically—I do have a fancy degree, you know. Relevant to your situation is the very nature of time. Time is a measurement of change. And we humans are time-bound. That is, everything we experience takes place over time. For us, time is always passing. Twenty years—or in your case, eight years—seems like a long time, looking forward, anyway, and not backward.

God is not time-bound. He exists outside of time. Therefore, whether something takes five minutes or five millennia is insignificant to God. Everything to him occurs in an ever present moment. As the theologians would say, "God lives in an eternal now."

In a sense, we share in God's time. All that is immediately "real" to us is the now. Our past exists only in memories; our future doesn't yet exist. We are beings who experience life as a long string of present moments. See, I do remember something from my college minor in philosophy, if only enough to muddle my head.

So how does all this metaphysical lingo help you? Said simply, what is long for you is not long for God. He's already heard your every prayer for your son, from your first to your someday last. Yet he obviously wants you to keep praying. He's said so repeatedly.

Jesus tells the parable of a "judge who neither feared God nor regarded man" (Luke 18:2). When a widow came seeking redress, the judge ignored her. Undeterred, she returned day after day until he finally answered her pleas. (See Luke 18:1–5)

The message is not that God is some lofty judge who only answers prayers if he's nagged enough. The message is: Persevere in prayer. God understands better than we do how important something is to us. He wants us to understand it better too—not only in mind but in action. Persistent prayer must be very good for both the pray-er and the pray-ee, or else God wouldn't tell us to do it.

Our Lord routinely linked prayer and faith. To use a popular phrase, "Faith is a muscle." It is a commitment to act. By ever praying, you are being ever faithful. You are behaving as a mother who will do all she can for her child's spiritual well-being.

Feeling weary is understandable. It is an all too human reaction when a deep longing seems to go unfulfilled. It is not, however, a sign of wearying faith.

Feelings are not the best guide to conduct. Your intent is to pray whether you feel like it or not. It is to seek God's guidance, whether you fathom it or not. Indeed, it is a great act of faith to pray on when nothing seems to be moved by your prayers.

Perhaps you will pray until the day you leave this earth, with your son still at a distance from God. What will you see from heaven? Changes in him you never saw on earth? Will your passing affect his soul, already softened by your many years of prayer? There is so much we can't foresee.

One more thought: Praying for another's conversion always interacts with his free will. God does not force himself on anyone. How he moves a soul remains a mystery. Still, he only needs the smallest opening to enter, one often created by a mother's prayers.

Dreaming of Sin

Dear Dr. Ray,

I've been having a recurrent dream in which I'm committing a serious sin. It's not anything I have actually done or would want to do. Could this be a sign of some unconscious desire to commit this sin?

—*Night Mary*

In psychology school, many of my waking hours were spent thinking about dreams. What are they? Why do they happen? What do they mean for the person having them?

In psychology's youth, dreams had a lot more status than they do today. Some argued that they told more about one's inner workings than did his waking moments. Freud called dreams the "royal road to the unconscious activities of the mind."[3] Because the psyche's defenses were half-asleep, so to speak, the stuff of one's forbidden desires and passions had a crack to poke through, although in a disguised form. Hence the need for trained interpreters of dreams.

Though most clinicians no longer follow Freud, some of his theories still reside in our culture's collective consciousness. The idea that dreams talk of one's inner life still lingers. It seems to be what's troubling you.

What is a dream? The brain mechanisms behind dreams are still poorly understood. Research posits that dreams are a peculiar hodge-podge of one's preoccupations, recent thoughts, bits and pieces of memories, prior days' events. Put another way, they are physiological stews that don't follow the laws of reality, as they flit erratically through associations, settings, and time.

What's more, to recall a dream or its parts, a person has to awaken during or shortly after it. When someone says, "I don't dream much," he's mistaken. Everybody dreams. What he's really saying is that he sleeps soundly, with little arousal during the night. All that potential psychological grist left untapped!

Why do dreams happen? Freud and his colleagues maintained that dreams serve the psyche. They light up the inner life of the person. That theory has pretty much fallen asleep. Presently dreams are thought to serve some brain function, though exactly what isn't clear. Perhaps they prune excess, unnecessary neural connections—redundancies, if you will. Or they simply reflect random brain activity, as the brain stays awake even while we're asleep. Whatever their cause, dreams don't appear to unlock hidden realities so much as they gather and muddle wide-awake ones.

What do dreams mean? This arouses the fascination of many people. What do my dreams say about me? Am I who I think I am, or could I be worse and not know it? This is the heart of your worry.

Why this particular dream for you? The answer might surprise you. Your dream may not be unmasking a desire to sin but just the opposite: It could reflect a strong desire *not* to sin. Your whole being shuns this sin, and your mind has twisted that rejection out of shape. People dream at least as much about what disturbs them as they do about what attracts them.

Perhaps you struggle with the reality that many people actually commit your dream's sin with no thought or guilt. Or perhaps this dream theme has been wired into your brain with repetition.

For years I've had a dream—nightmare—that is common to former college students. I'm back in school, it's late in the semester, and not only have I not once opened the textbook, but I haven't attended any classes. As I sit in the course for the very first time, I'm staring at an exam, totally clueless. Of course, my college days did offer some courses that found me clueless, but I studied my way through them. How come that part is never in my dream?

Why this dream now? At thirty-plus years post-college, I'm not about to reenroll, so I can't flunk out. I suspect the dream is an exaggeration of a once-upon-a-time worry that my brain has wired for replay. Upon waking up, I usually relive my relief of graduation day. But now I am a little nervous that writing about this will prompt a rerun tonight.

Which prompts my advice for you. Try not to be distressed about your dream. If it bothers you in the day, it's more likely to bother you at night. Don't fear the dream, and it will lose power. Take a shrug-your-shoulders attitude toward it. Worrying about another one tonight may be the very emotion that spurs the dream.

Can dreams ever be occasions of sin? I'm not a moral theologian, but Morality 101 teaches that serious sin involves a conscious act of the will. An individual must know something is a serious sin and then deliberately choose to do it anyway. Anything that interferes with free choice reduces the personal blame attached to a wrong.

A dream can be an occasion of sin, indirectly. An individual can desire the dream and take wide-awake pleasure in having had it. He can look forward to its next visit. He can use it as fodder for daydreaming—that is, relive the forbidden act in his mind while avoiding any real-life complications.

In essence, a dream can allow someone to do something in fantasy that he wouldn't do in life. Given your dream distress, none of these would seem to be a concern.

To repeat, you cannot sin while you're asleep. Dreams are random physiological phenomena rather than windows to the soul. What a dream says matters little when compared to how we live when awake.

Holier Pre-Kid

Dear Dr. Ray,
Before I had children, I saw myself as a calm, easygoing person. Three kids later, I have a new self-image—a not so pretty one. I get upset more easily, scold more, and overall have to work harder to control my emotions. I think I could go to confession every day.
—Uneven Tempered

Children are precious gifts of God, of infinite worth. They deserve all the love we have to give them. None of which necessarily means that they are easy to live with. How easy is it to live with someone who is immature, self-focused, resistant to rules, and guided by a juvenile conscience? The profile sounds unattractive, but it describes the natural state of most children, particularly younger ones.

At the very heart of the Christian understanding of humans is our fallen nature. We are all born with a bent toward self, toward rebellion—indeed toward sin. As G.K. Chesterton so astutely observed, the Christian doctrine of original sin is "the only part of Christian theology which can really be proved."[4]

Only with heavenly grace do we begin the lifelong process of turning our self-will toward God's will. You know the struggle; you revealed so in your question. And you're an adult, with years of maturity, experience, self-examination, and motive to conquer your self. Even were you raising the most sweet, cooperative, loving children, you'd still have your imperfect nature to deal with in raising them.

Fallen nature is at its most unruly at its youngest. That's why children desperately need parents to help them mature out of their natural ways. The whole process of socializing and moralizing one's offspring takes the better part of two decades, with all kinds of surprises and emotional jolts and plenty of annoyance along the way. How could frustration not intrude? How could you never raise your voice or say regrettable things? How could you not sin?

For most parents, the rewards far outweigh the hassles (especially looking back!). But there may be plenty of hassles which can be near occasions of sin. It is so much easier to be good when you don't share a roof with others—big or little. One saint, upon visiting her sister with many children, is reported to have remarked on her need to get back to the convent, where it was quieter, with less temptation to irritation.

It's an old axiom: You only hurt the ones you love. Perhaps it's better said: You hurt more the ones you love, and they you. Sad but true. Those we deeply love have the most potential to move us, for good or ill.

It's not much of a challenge for me to love all the people in Australia. As far as I know, not one of them has ever done anything to personally make my life difficult. My sons and daughters? Now, that's a whole different terrain. They reside only twenty to fifty feet from me most days, and they also inhabit the innermost precincts of my emotions. They can set the conditions for me to sin more than all of Australia, India, and China combined, throwing in Bolivia and Iceland to boot.

Before becoming a parent, most people dramatically underestimate the feelings a child can evoke. Whenever you are soaked in positive emotions, you are vulnerable to negative ones—irritation, disappointment, anger. So much do you want it to all go well, that when it doesn't, well...

One good definition of frustration: Frustration is the difference between the way we want things to be and the way they are. The bigger the gap, the more the frustration. To reduce frustration, it is generally easier to move our expectations closer to reality than to move reality closer to us.

Kids are kids. Am I profound or what? Reality says that they act far from our expectations for them, in the near years anyway. Living within this reality will lower your frustration, along with your temptation to act out that frustration.

I am not advising you to accept sin as a partner of parenthood. Obviously, you don't want to act your worst with your kids. My advice is to not be discouraged by the three steps forward two steps back trek to calmer, more even-tempered motherhood. Yes, you will sin. But over time you will likely sin less, especially as your kids move out.

In the meantime, here's what works for me: On the refrigerator, post an updated list of all the confession times at all the parishes in the diocese. Or keep a priest on call twenty-four hours.

Section Six

Family Friction

It's an axiom of life: Those closest to us have the most emotional power to move us, for better or worse. And for most people, those closest are family. It is disheartening when our deepest held beliefs are a source of frustration, even friction, between us and those we love.

Continuing to love past religious differences and speaking the truth gently will gradually bridge family divides. They may even lead to a meeting of minds and hearts.

Don't Force It

Dear Dr. Ray,

My daughter and her husband have two children, ages five and three. They are not raising the kids in the Church, as they were raised. When I try to pass on to my grandchildren some of the most basic faith practices—praying before meals, taking them to Mass when they are with me, giving them picture Bibles—my daughter gets upset and tells me I'm pushing my religion on her family.

—*Silenced Grandma*

Adult children who leave the faith of their childhood are an ongoing source of disappointment, and often self-reproach, for their parents. What happened to your daughter on her way from your family to hers? How did she jettison the core of what you taught her all those years? And will she ever embrace it again?

Whatever your second-guessing is over raising her, it is now intensified by watching your daughter raise her kids. Do you somehow feel responsible for your own supposed failures in parenting being passed on to a second generation? If so, guilt over the past can push you hard to correct the present.

Your daughter's faith loss, however, does not necessarily reflect how faithfully she was raised. Many factors influence someone's choices about God. (See "Two Out of Three?" in section eight.)

However good your intentions in trying to pass on the faith to your grandchildren, you face a major obstacle: Your daughter doesn't agree. Her resistance may not be so much about your religion as about her parenting, specifically about her motherhood and its perceived deficiencies. She reads your wanting to say meal blessings with the kids as your way to fill in her family's religious gaps.

Yes, you are Grandma, but she is Mom. However misguided you believe she is, she has the right to parent her own children. By teaching against her will, not only could you antagonize her, but you could push her and her husband further from the faith. Your daughter might also limit your access to the kids if she sees no other way to restrain you. Softening your daughter's attitude is difficult, if not impossible, if she feels you are ignoring or defying her.

Therefore, my suggestion is to cease your religious guidance. Apologize to your daughter and husband for not respecting their wishes. Assure them also that you will never do anything with which they would disagree. To make any religious inroads, you must first have a solid relationship. It's the base from which you may one day be able to teach freely.

What about your Christian call to share the faith? You can't impose something that isn't wanted. What if the kids want it? Even so, their mother doesn't, and she is deciding for them, right now anyway.

And you can still teach your grandchildren the faith. How? Be loving and easy to get along with. The children—and their mother—will see Grandma as a really neat religious lady. The combination is winsome.

Through it all, don't get discouraged. Many adult children return to the Church as they come to realize the worth of giving their own children something more than this world's philosophy. The kids lead them home.

Forbidden Fruit

Dear Dr. Ray,

Our sixteen-year-old daughter is smitten with an eighteen-year-old boy whom my husband and I know to be a troubled young man. I want to curtail their contact, but my husband says to let things run their course or we'll just make the relationship a forbidden fruit.

—Swallowing Hard

Biblical in its imagery, *forbidden fruit* has come to mean "something that looks pleasing because it is denied." Even if that something is not healthy for us, we want it because we can't have it.

Our first parents had the pick of nearly anything in Paradise. The whole garden was theirs to enjoy, with one exception. The tree that God commanded them to leave alone, they didn't. They tasted its fruit, with world-altering repercussions.

We, their descendants were wounded morally by their disobedience and are thus attracted to much we should leave alone. When we see this inclination in our descendants—our children—we worry. By forbidding something they desire, will we make it all the more desirable?

Out-of-reach fruit may look the sweetest, especially to young eyes. Someone with more mature eyes (read "parent") must sometimes declare it unpickable. The child's very well-being demands it.

Parents have to make all manner of judgments over the years, guided by what is good for a child, not by how much she wants it or could react if denied it. A five-year-old craves sugar-loaded cereal for breakfast. Deny him, and you wonder if you'll start him on the path to a calorie-crazed adulthood stuffed with jumbo, jelly-filled donuts. A fourteen-year-old daughter is absolutely desperate to spend time with the older neighbor boy, at his house, alone. Will a nonnegotiable "No way" only push her to the limits of sneakiness? A college sophomore living at home sees no problem whatsoever to his sampling vile video games. Will your refusal to acquiesce drive him deeper into virtual unreality, if not at your house then someday at his?

Much that looks ever so delicious to children will make them sick. A parent must decide what fruit to allow when and how much. Rare is the child who never needs protection from his appetites. And where these appetites threaten morals and character, a parent has to act with steadfastness. She can't be paralyzed by the fear of creating some forbidden fruit.

Dad wants to let the relationship run its course. To where? And who's driving? Can you know how it all will end? Who could get hurt on its way forward or backward? As my grandmother would say, "Better you cry now than we both cry later."

Your husband may have faith that your daughter will eventually see this young man as you do. Maybe so, but again, at what cost? What complications could arise in the meantime? The course a teen chooses is not always wise or safe.

Much farsighted parenting involves having a plan B. Your husband likely will agree with it, your daughter, likely not—though she may be forced to accept it if she sees it as her only option. Here's a possible plan B: Allow limited, closely supervised boy-girl contact, with you and Dad as the supervisors. Of necessity, this would happen at your home or perhaps on a double date, with you and Dad as the doubles.

Plan B has two upsides. One, in a morally protected setting, your daughter will have time to better digest the character of this relationship. Two, this young man may seek other gardens, having decided you are a bit too forbidding for his tastes.

My belly tells me the latter will happen before the former.

Too Many Channels

Dear Dr. Ray,

My father lets my sons, ages ten and twelve, watch television shows at his house that I would never approve of. He argues, "It's not going to hurt them."

—*A Different View*

"It's not going to hurt them" comes with some standard companions: "It's not like they're going to be violent criminals." "That's real life—they'll see lots of it." "You can't shelter them forever." "They're good kids—they can handle it."

To this last one, one mother answered, "I think they're good kids too, and I'd like to keep them that way."

In teaching virtue, the guiding principle is not "What harm will it do?" It is "What good will it do?" We humans can survive all manner of threats and assaults. That doesn't mean they are good for us. Most of the time, the body neutralizes life-endangering germs. Are such germs then of no concern?

When I was fourteen, I fell face-first down a flight of stairs while carrying two folding chairs under each arm. (Macho teen boy, anyone?) I didn't touch anything until I hit the concrete floor. Yet except for a bruised ego, I walked away unscathed. Did this demonstrate that similar future shortcuts would pose no risk to me?

"It won't hurt them" can be a rationale for indifference. It can be a way of saying, "It takes too much effort to supervise this." If I can convince myself that kids are naturally resilient to technological toxins, I won't have to be quite so vigilant. And I won't have to weather their upset over my rules.

Your dilemma is not caused by your father's thinking. He can have his opinion; you don't have to abide by it. He may believe that he needs to give the boys some cultural normalcy because their parents don't. He must compensate for your overprotectiveness. If you're going to be out of step with the majority, he won't be.

Your dilemma is caused by your father's behavior. Whether intending to or not, he is sending his grandkids the message, "Your parents are wrong; I'll correct it when you're with me." Not only is he undercutting you at his place, but he's making life tougher for you at yours. Your sons could resent the fact that you aren't as TV-cool as Grandpa. After all, he's a grown-up too, and one who has been around a lot longer than you. He should know more about this TV thing.

How much have you talked with your dad about why you raise the boys as you do? Not just your television stance but overall? How clear have you been? Does he understand that TV monitoring is one of your nonnegotiables?

He doesn't have to agree, just cooperate. How can you confirm that he does? Without being in Grandpa's house, you can't. He and the boys could form a sort of viewer's conspiracy. Your ally, however, is time.

Kids aren't the best at keeping secrets secret for very long. The truth will be broadcast in their actions. Watch for any acting out of the pictures they've seen. Listen for vocabulary foreign to your home but native to TV.

Should Grandpa insist on offering multiple cable channels, no matter your pleas, he has boxed you into a corner. You may have to figure out how to supervise not only your sons but your father. This may mean only visiting Grandpa as a family. Or one parent could always accompany the boys. It's too bad when a parent has to take such steps, but your father is forcing you to—that is, unless you are willing to discard your standards.

"Honor thy father and mother" means we must give parents the respect and love that are their due. It does not mean that you, as an adult, have to abide by their every request and decision. Nor does your approach to raising children have to be in line with theirs.

Others don't always agree with good parenting. And sometimes those others are our own parents.

Whatever happened to the days when grandparents only sneaked the kids a second helping of ice cream? After they finished their cookie.

Whom Do You Trust?

Dear Dr. Ray,

We supervise our daughter socially far more than her friends' parents do their children. She routinely says, "You just don't trust me." We need an answer.

—*The Hawks*

How short an answer do you want? How about, "I trust you; I don't trust the world." If you want something longer, I'll give it. I suspect, though, that your daughter probably won't accept it any better than my pithy sound bite.

You could say, "Oh, but I do trust you. I trust that you are fifteen. And I trust that fifteen-year-olds think like fifteen-year-olds. And I trust that there will be situations that, for all your wisdom, you'll be unsure how to handle. And I trust that with time, I'll allow you to experience more. And I trust that you'll believe me when I tell you I'm doing this out of love and to protect you, as a most precious gift from God."

Tell me, how could she not be moved by such an open expression of trust?

If, after all this, your daughter still wants to call your vigilance a lack of trust, so be it. It's not that you don't respect her level of maturity. It's that you understand fully her youth. Don't allow her to make you feel guilty by turning a positive (sound parental judgment) into a negative (a personal insult).

Why are kids so quick to take our loving suggestions personally? For one, humans in general are quick to take another's behavior personally. Call it the sensitivity of the self.

For another, teens in particular are quick to misunderstand parents' motives. To them what you are doing stems from your inability to see them accurately. You just don't realize yet how trustworthy and downright grown-up they are. In short, the problem, dear parent, lies in your misperception, not in their youth.

Another reason kids freely fling the "You just don't trust me" accusation is this: It may be true; you don't fully trust them. And so? Incomplete trust isn't a bad thing, socially or psychologically. It's recognizing reality. Indeed, a wise parent realizes the limits of a child's judgment, experience, and character. Even the most mature fifteen-year-old is still a fifteen-year-old.

Other parents might fuel your daughter's fire. How? By letting their kids do too much too soon. As your daughter sees it, if all those grown-ups give more so-called trust than you, you are the suspicious one. How could all of them be wrong and you alone be right? If this were a game, the score would be twenty-three (other parents) to two (you and your spouse).

Here you face your toughest battle with your daughter. You know—and I hope you act by your knowledge—that even if the score were 123 parents to you, it would be irrelevant. Good parenting is never done by group vote. The question is not, how do my standards compare to others? The question is, how do my standards reflect the kind of child I wish to raise?

If you believe your daughter's friends have far too much freedom for their age, then you must parent differently—sometimes radically so. Your daughter won't always understand you. Someday she will, and that's what really matters.

For now, the only foolproof way to convince your daughter that you do trust her is to give her all the freedom she wishes. But it's not worth the price.

To Love, Not Condone

Dear Dr. Ray,

At age twenty-one, my daughter moved in with her boyfriend. My husband and I didn't raise her to think that is moral. It's been over a year, and I'm still uneasy around them.
—*Troubled*

How uneasy are you, and how much does your daughter—her boyfriend too—sense it? Are your times together tense, and consequently, are there less of them? The natural course of an uneasy relationship is toward dwindling contact.

I believe you wish to stay close to your daughter, even as she continues to stay so close to her boyfriend. I also believe you wish to send no message condoning their housekeeping. How do you balance these seemingly competing aims?

To put it more broadly: How does one love another without accepting his wrong conduct? A profound question, it is one that forces itself upon Christians repeatedly throughout life.

Above all, we are called to love, to treat others—the moral and the not so—with dignity and decency. We are also called to live by clear-cut standards, not formed by our own opinions but by the revelation of God. And these standards are not solely for the benefit of believers but for all people.

At any time, for any reason, anyone can choose to neglect or reject God's standards and expect us to accept, even esteem, that choice. It's an irony that someone can ask, often demand, that others be tolerant of whatever moral position she takes but will be most intolerant of their moral position about her moral position.

Your daughter knows exactly what you believe. No doubt, you've told her in one way or another throughout the past year. And you raised her with your beliefs for another twenty years prior to that. It's not that she doesn't understand and only needs more instruction. It's that, for the time anyway, she's chosen to live counter to those beliefs.

Therefore, no longer broach the matter. Should your daughter do so, then the door is open. If you are the one to reopen it, you'll accomplish little other than to open up more emotional distance between you. Conversations take on a stiffness when one or more parties anticipate a touchy subject lurking just around the next sentence. Remove the verbal risk, and you'll remove some two-way uneasiness.

Could your daughter hear your reticence as acceptance? Shouldn't you say something every few visits or so, just to remind her that you're not growing indifferent to her playing house? Couldn't she get the impression that her arrangement is all right by you?

Not likely. You have too much shared history for that.

Suppose, however, that she does conclude that your moral vision is blurring. After all, she would probably like you more on her side in this. Even then, you are under no moral obligation to reiterate your stance endlessly. You are only responsible to communicate it, and you have done that over the years. You are not responsible for your daughter misreading why you no longer communicate it.

The religious leaders of our Lord's day censured him because he ate with tax collectors, who were considered among the most despicable of sinners. Dining at the same table wasn't seen as a mere social get-together; it bespoke deep fellowship. Scripture doesn't report Jesus admonishing, "OK, guys, don't think any of this means I approve of what you're doing. And you've got two weeks to forsake it, or you won't be seeing me around here anymore." No, the sinners and everybody else knew where Jesus stood on their conduct; nonetheless, he continued to reach out to them.

Your love for your daughter—and her boyfriend—is your best means to morally move them. Without a decent relationship, you won't have much of a chance to persuade. Understandably, her living arrangement causes discomfort for you, and understandably, you might have to fake being relaxed around her, but in the end both of you will be rewarded. Whether one day she and her boyfriend break up, marry, or separate domiciles, you want your personal bridge to her to remain solid, without any lingering resentments toward you. And you don't want her to carry over and attitude that says, "Oh, now you're going to be warm toward me because I'm good again."

While you pray for your daughter's change of heart, pray too that your heart never changes toward her.

The College Experience

Dear Dr. Ray,

Our daughter graduates from high school this year. She is adamant about living on a college campus, and the farther away, the better. She wants the "college experience." My wife and I have strong reservations about this. We'd prefer she attend college nearby and live at home.

—Experienced Dad

Some thirty-plus years ago, I had the college experience, nearly a decade's worth. Did I rush into freedom? Face first. Did I come, go, sleep, wake on my own cycle? Sure did. Did I chase fun? Yep. Did my religion become more self-defined? Afraid so.

In the 1970s, my college persona was the norm. Today it wouldn't be. It would be seen as a little too restrained.

Not many would dispute that the college social scene has decayed in just one generation. Alcohol, drugs, sex, parties, rock and roll—all are attending school in greater numbers alongside the students. Some kids pilot through the shoals and graduate afloat. Many—surveys say half or more—pass their courses but flunk the morals and faith taught for years by their families.

Once upon a time, institutes of higher learning wore the mantle of *in loco parentis* ("in place of the parent" for those of you who overslept Latin class). They took seriously their part in guiding and supervising young adults. Many schools now seem to practice *in absentia parentis*. They ally with the students, not with the parents. They let young people discover—some would say "stumble"—their way forward. The results of this philosophical shift have not been pretty.

All this is not to paint a bleak and scary picture. It's to sketch a real one for parents as a teen nears college.

If you lived on campus back when, don't use your experience, however maturing, to predict your daughter's. Because you landed upright (Does your wife want to gather the relatives and vote on that?), you can't assume your daughter will too. The numbers tell of a changing reality.

"But she really wants to go." No doubt. But as my little sister used to retort when we argued, "So?" Children really want all kinds of things—some good, some real bad. A parent has to help them decide which is which and sometimes has to make the decision for them. You can't foresee your daughter's future, so you're forced to make a judgment call. Do kids like parents' judgment calls? Only those in their favor.

You have "strong reservations." Is one of them related to your daughter's level of maturity and trustworthiness? The best predictor of future behavior is past behavior in similar situations. Your daughter hasn't yet lived on a campus; she has lived in a far more supervised setting—home. How has she done?

Some kids can be trusted solo on a Bahamian cruise. Others, not in the next room. How your daughter has behaved the last few years is one good gauge of how she'll behave in the next few.

In addition to moral and social questions, there is an economic one: Who is the bank? You? Even partially? This gives you a veto vote in her college choice. But perhaps your daughter will pay for everything—tuition, room and board, books, insurance, car, cell phone, curling iron, whatever. As a legal-aged adult, she can thus attend where she chooses.

My oldest daughter, Hannah, was attracted to a leadership training curriculum at an all-female college out of state. Knowing our position—you live here, we pay; you live there, you pay (no loans)—she enrolled in ROTC at the college, graduating as an officer in the army, her desired career. Three of our other children attended universities within commuting distance. All four graduated with a priceless life lesson: "No loans is good."

Speaking of money, statistics indicate that up to half of college graduates are not working in their chosen major. Many find jobs that barely cover living expenses, much less loan payments stretching as far as their eyes can see. For several years, they enjoyed faux-independence, only to find themselves moving back to dependence—Mom and Dad's place. Their youth made them financially shortsighted. You are older and more clear-eyed about money matters.

A college-near-home stance could meet exceptions. Certain technical or specialized degrees might only be available beyond commuting distance. Generous scholarship awards from colleges are a draw. Catholic and other private traditional schools may offer a solid faith-building and moral education, a college experience that would move with you rather than against you.

Your instincts are pushing you hard in one direction. Your daughter is pushing you hard in another. When a parent ignores or suppresses his strong instincts, one reason is fear of a child's reaction. Will she be resentful? Will she rebel? Will she move out? (Is that a problem?)

All could happen—in most cases, temporarily—but none justify allowing something that you believe is unwise.

The New Moral Normal

It's an ongoing tug of war. At one end are those who assert, "This is the way the world now is. Children have to learn how to live in it." At the other end are those who counter, "Children need more time to morally mature before having to learn how to live in it."

So who sets the pace for learning? Society with its ever-lowering standards? Or a child's parent, who in slowing the pace and protecting innocence may feel increasingly out of rhythm with society?

Conventional thinking says: Kids have to navigate the world as it now is. Conventional thinking isn't always reliable wisdom.

Protective Parents

Dear Dr. Ray,

My four children are all under age eleven. Others have called me a protective parent, and it's not typically meant as a compliment. I just don't want my kids growing up too fast.

—*Mama Lion*

By "protective" I assume you don't mean that you shield your children from all the natural, age-related fallout of their conduct. You're not driving an emotional bulldozer in front of them, clearing their lives of every rock and bump. Instead, you mean that you want to give them a few more years of childhood and a few less years of premature adulthood.

Modern child-raising theories have turned much of the wisdom of the past on its head. Not so long ago, the view was that parents should indeed "overprotect" their children, not only from lions and tigers and bears but from the dangers of seeing too much worldly ugliness too early. Childhood innocence was a treasure to be guarded and nurtured.

Only recently have those who resist society's rush to socialize at young ages been questioned, scorned even, as if they were stunting their children's social growth. "You can't protect them forever." "That's a tough world out there." "They've got to learn to deal with life."

No, you can't protect them forever. Yes, the world is tough. And yes, children do have to deal with it. But I know few parents who want to shelter their children always and everywhere, keeping them holed up socially until Independence Day. They want to shelter them—emotionally and morally—longer than the new cultural norm says to.

Anytime the word *protection* is used, the question naturally follows: Protection from what, when, and for how long? As a parent, the answer is all yours. Others—including many so-called experts—will push you to move along with the crowd's pace. But a wise parent sets the pace based upon the family's values and the child's moral maturity.

Much that is supposedly normal—normal according to society that is—is not necessarily good. The majority of teens have televisions in their bedrooms. Nearly all thirteen-year-olds have cell phones. Most kids drive the day their age allows. Are these norms we should automatically follow because the numbers say so? How did they become the guide to virtue?

Protective is also a relative term. One could legitimately argue that the most sheltered ten-year-old of today has seen and heard more social pollution than the typical fourteen-year-old of three generations ago. Back then, you wouldn't have been called "protective"; you would have been called responsible. Could it be that you're not overprotective but look so compared to those who are underprotective?

The idea is widespread: Children are faced with new adult realities, so they'd best face them sooner rather than later—helped by grown-ups, of course. The assumption is that somehow one is better able to adjust if he adjusts at a young age. He'll have more years to learn to cope. Some child-rearing notions I can only respond to with a definite "Huh?"

Who is more suited to navigate moral trickiness—a well-raised ten-year-old or a well-raised fourteen-year-old? The relationship is basic: The older the child, the more internal resources he has to handle what comes at him. Postponing the day of moral and emotional testing does not arrest a child's development; it gives us time to strengthen the child for the test.

The next time someone accuses you of being a protective parent—code for overprotective parent—you might answer, "You're right. I try to be. I want to give my kids a childhood while they're still children."

Teach Me about This, Mom

Dear Dr. Ray,

My brother tells me I should let my children watch morally borderline TV shows so I can use them as "teachable moments." Have you heard this phrase?

—Uneducated

As childrearing lingo goes, *teachable moment* is as broad as it is trendy. It refers to using a situation, experience, or problem to teach a child something worthwhile. It means drawing a good lesson from some life event, good or bad.

Good parents teach to the moment all the time. They take advantage of openings to instruct or correct. For example, Mom and little Rocky are watching a cartoon about a car-eating space invader. (Whatever happened to simple good and bad guys, like Popeye and Bluto?) Assuming she can wrest Rocky's attention from the TV for six seconds, Mom can slip in a question or two to help him see the story with a more mature moral eye. Used this way, teachable moments are a parent's ally in forming character.

Your brother is stretching the concept. He advises exposing your children to something questionable so you can ask questions about it. Really, he's saying, "Let's talk about how what you're watching is not good for you."

Most sensory input enters through the eyes. At any instant, we see much more than we hear. Words matter, but as the most novice ad person knows, the vision can outtalk the best of slogans.

"One picture is worth a thousand words." For most of its history, this adage referred to basic, two-dimensional reproductions. Our ancestors revered the power of images, even back when they were very imperfect reflections of reality. Today, with computer-created anything and high-definition, rocket-paced television, one could assert, "One picture is worth a million words." Our techno world has fashioned images that seem more real than reality itself.

An extreme illustration is pornography. A devastating effect of viewing pornography is that the pictures are seared into the mind's eye, becoming tenacious residents of one's storehouse of memories. It is far better never to have experienced these images than to try to delete them with after-the-moment discussions. Even with the best professional counseling, this can be an uphill slog.

This reveals the serious flaw in the teaching-moment concept. The more intensely negative an image or experience, the less we can draw something positive from it.

Some people advocate a more moderate stance: Create teachable moments but not recklessly. Don't throw children into the deep end of life's pool. Let them wade into shallow water holding your hand.

Still, cautions are warranted. For one, a parent might not want her child to get wet yet. She knows the pool will still be open when her child is a better swimmer. No need to venture into deeper water just to teach the child that it's deep.

For another, how a particular moment will affect a particular child is hard to anticipate. Two siblings can react quite differently to the same experience. Storm weathers it with little afterthought, while Sunny bakes in it for the next three hours, cries himself to sleep, and has dark dreams for a week straight. The only way to know for sure how teachable a moment will be is to let it happen. And that might prove costly.

Here is my teaching for the moment. Don't let your children be exposed to anything you think will be premature, given their ages and innocence. Every parent has limitless teaching opportunities without adding any that will force her to teach something before its time.

Too often, the teachable moment is a smart-sounding rationale for yielding to the culture's pace of shoving adulthood at children.

Rebellion Risk?

Dear Dr. Ray,

We're a young family trying to raise our children with strong morals. We've been told that if our standards are too high, our kids will rebel.

—*Highly Skeptical*

Your standards are too high? How do you measure that? Can you poll a hundred people for a consensus? And what if your desire to live right is stronger than most?

The only way, it seems, to judge if you're pushing your family's moral bar out of reach is to watch whether your kids try to jump for it or limbo under it. Then you'll know. Not really, as we will see shortly.

"High standards" is not an absolute phrase. It is a relative one. A standard can look extreme when compared to a group standard that has slipped. These days, many people measure moral correctness by what is seen as the norm. That is, normal is right. If the norm is unhealthy, however, then what is healthy can seem abnormal.

The notion that high standards risk rebellion has gotten lots of momentum from the professionals. (Just because someone gets paid for giving advice doesn't mean the advice is always good.) Recently I attended a meeting where one therapist, whose specialty was adolescents, proclaimed authoritatively, "We all know that all teens will rebel if a parent's standards are too high." Were I feeling more rebellious, I would have countered, "No, we don't all know that, and all teens won't rebel." Call it my inner adolescent.

The therapist's warning is one of those sophisticated new insights that have overturned long-standing, everyday wisdom. Not so long ago, the belief was that the higher the standards, the better. It was a lack of strong standards that led to poor living. Of late, we've learned the supposed reverse: High standards can lead to poor living.

This fallacy underlies the stereotype of the preacher's kid. Everyone knows that the most morally unprincipled kid in the whole congregation is the preacher's. Saying yes to his dad's teaching, he says no to living it and tries to fly low under the parental radar.

What "everyone knows," though, turns out to be more often false than true. The exception has given birth to the rule. In fact, most preachers' kids grow up to reflect, not reject, their upbringing. And of those who do reject it, many one day return to the morals learned in youth.

Jesus said, "You...must be perfect, as your heavenly Father is perfect" (Matthew 5:48). Perfect? Such a non-negotiable word. Was Jesus teaching that the only path to heaven lies in keeping impossibly high precepts? Or was he encouraging us to stretch toward those precepts?

More than anyone, Jesus understood the frailty of fallen human nature. He also knew that, because of our frailty, we need clear guiding ideals.

How does a parent lower a moral bar that she worries is too high? "You should always tell the truth, Truman, but 'always' does seem a bit demanding, so how about a maximum of two lies a week, three if they're small." "Always treat your sister with respect, Justice, but if you feel you can't, at least try not to curse at her." "We realize, Chastity, that our 'no dating until seventeen' rule is stricter than most other parents'. So you can start texting relationships at age fourteen."

To compromise a standard, one has to allow exceptions to it. And the exceptions weaken its spirit.

As we've said elsewhere, many young adults today are forsaking, at least in part, their parents' moral teachings. This is often thought to be a sign that the kids couldn't meet family expectations; therefore, they renounced them. An understandable reaction. This interpretation is often wrong. Grown children leave the faith for myriad reasons—cultural forces preeminent. Shedding the yoke of binding standards is not high on the list.

Kids rebel against standards that they neither fully understand nor appreciate. Young minds routinely judge the most reasonable principles as too demanding or unjust. That's because most kids survey what their peers are allowed to do and think, "How can all those parents be wrong and my parents be right?" Only when they look back with adult vision, especially that magnified by raising their own children, do they come to realize how right their parents were.

That being said, it is important to provide guidance lovingly. As Josh McDowell, a Christian author and speaker, says, "Rules without relationship breed rebellion."[5] A rigid code of conduct enforced with little love and affection is asking for resistance. It can be seen as a "my way or the highway" ruling style rather than benevolent guidance.

High standards are most durably imparted when wrapped in spoken and unspoken "I love yous." When a child feels valued, he's far more open to values.

Remember, too, your children are not walking the higher moral plane all alone. You're walking with them. Your standards are not only for the little people but for the big people as well. Everybody is raised up by high standards.

Beyond the Three R's

Dear Dr. Ray,

My fifth-grade daughter's health class has an upcoming one-week section on sexual education. I've looked at the material, and it is very explicit, especially for a ten-year-old. It also presents a moral perspective far different from our own. Options?
—Prudish Parent

Once upon a time, on a planet far away, schools concentrated on shaping young minds through the three R's—reading, 'riting, and 'rithmetic. Education in attitudes, morals, and character was recognized as subjects for the parents' classroom. Schools could assist, but only within the framework of the family.

Nowadays, a new letter is added to the scholastic alphabet. We now have the three S's—Safe sex, Save the earth, and Say no to drugs. And these letters don't always spell good words for parents, particularly parents who are more traditionally religious.

Two plus two equals four. The speed of light is 186,000 miles per second. Babe Ruth was the greatest baseball player of all time. These are indisputable truths. (All right, maybe it's Mickey Mantle.) One can disagree with them only if he wishes to dispute reality.

On the other hand, teaching when, how, and with whom to have sexual relations; presenting the perils of cocaine; discerning whether a five-child family is hogging a disproportionate share of the earth's oxygen—these are matters of moral judgment, some-times scientific debate. And the best age for their introduction varies widely from child to child.

It is argued that, though such questions are best answered at home, too many homes ignore them. For good or ill, the task then falls to the schools, the next line of socialization. Sadly, there is truth to this. Some parents are more than content to let the schools teach not only the three R's but the three S's as well. Even so, plenty of mothers and fathers want to instill their own family's values and not those espoused by a textbook, especially a textbook with a decidedly antireligious worldview.

Another argument: Schools need to form the whole child—that is, teach him not just how to read and write but how to think right. If thinking right means training in logic and reason, I couldn't agree more. But if it means instruction in a new and better way to live, I couldn't agree less. Who decides what is new and better? Who decides what it means to think right morally? An author? An expert? An atheist? Or a parent, with the God-given responsibility to teach what is right—that is, what she believes is the best way for her child to live?

On to your particular dilemma. First step: Pull together the textbook's more controversial or offensive passages, as you see them—on one page if possible. Show them to any other parents you think would be interested in reading up close what their ten- or eleven-year-olds are expected to read and hear about. Likely many, if not most, will be unaware of the topics and planned guidance.

Next, meet with the teacher, the principal, or both. Most educators are open to a parent's concerns. However, most are not open to rearranging subject matter because of one voice. If other parents are with you, your voice will echo.

Don't verbally pounce. Don't dispute—not at the moment you walk in the door, anyway. As reasonable as your points might be, you'll risk sounding unreasonable and invite a credibility problem.

You are there first to ask questions, to hear the school's rationale. Why is this subject matter presented at this grade level? What if the values conveyed are different from a parent's? Are there ways to keep a student innocent about these topics a while longer?

The administrator might understand, even agree, with your perspective but not have the authority to alter the curriculum. Likewise, the teacher could be sympathetic; perhaps he or she also thinks the material is questionable and, after hearing from you or others, might find ways to teach it at a level more age-suitable. Having the principal and teacher philosophically allied with you almost always makes a solution easier to work out.

Whether the school agrees with you or not, it will probably look for a compromise. For example, your daughter might be permitted to quietly slip out of class to another place: the library, cafeteria, office, or study hall. If the principal or teacher doesn't suggest this, you can. As the parent, you have the final authority.

One person left to consider is your daughter. While she may be thrilled to skip health class, she may not like looking like the social oddball. No matter how low-profile her exit, other kids may take note of her absence every day, same time and same subject. Any snide remarks about little Miss Purity and Mrs. Purity, her saintly mother, could talk your daughter into staying in her seat. And she might not read from the same page as you do.

To anticipate this, explain to your daughter something like, "There are things that are not appropriate for you to study at your age. And some of the instruction the school offers in these matters goes against what we believe as a family. As your mom and dad, we have to judge what is good for you to know and when.

"Next week, your health class will be teaching some subjects that we don't believe are right for you at age ten. So we've set it up with your teacher that you will leave class during that time and go to another place in the school. Questions?"

Clear. Rational. Sensitive. You should receive, "Oh, Mother, I was hoping you'd say this. I do so wish to stay a child longer, and I recognize that your way is the best way, even if all my friends and their parents think otherwise."

OK, back to earth. Should your daughter be upset with the arrangement, repeat your mini-speech every morning and evening until she agrees. Just joshing. Don't over-explain. Don't debate. Just make it happen. You are looking out for your daughter's long-term health.

The good news? Your daughter will probably stay upset only for the next week or so. Then she'll start asking what other classes she can escape.

May I Skip This Dance?

Dear Dr. Ray,
My son's school is holding its annual dance for eighth-graders. His mother and I think he's too young to go. We're surprised at the pressure on us to relent, not only from our son but from friends and others at the school.
—Dancing Solo

Some years ago, a dating survey of middle- and high-school students revealed that a child whose first date came between ages eleven and thirteen had a 90 percent chance of becoming sexually active by senior year. A first date at age fourteen: 50 percent chance of sexual activity senior year. First date at sixteen: 20 percent. There's a straight-line correlation: The earlier a child is introduced to one-on-one dating, the faster he progresses to full physical relations.

When I present these numbers to parent groups, the gasps are audible. The predominant thought: "Who would let a child date so young?" To which I answer, "Many, if not most, middle schools and junior highs sponsor dances."

One could argue that these dances aren't really dates but supervised get-togethers. Even so, they are early forays into the dating scene. And why wouldn't some kids push to use the dance as a date? After all, the school set it up. What's the problem?

Admittedly, the chances of a boy-girl stealthy tryst in such a setting may be low, assuming the adult supervision is high. Some would thus claim that these dances are safe exposure to the opposite sex. This would seem a variant of mis-thinking, "What's the harm?"

In forming morals, the guiding query is not "What's the harm?" but "What is the good?" Is low risk a good reason to encourage something that (for other reasons) is happening too soon?

Once upon a time, group socials were a natural step toward courting. The contact was communal, the dance partners were older than twelve, and the grown-ups made sure that first contacts were kept innocent. These days, anyone overseeing a supposedly innocent junior-high dance is forced to admit that the apparel itself is anything but innocent.

To which I hear the response, "It's not anything they don't see elsewhere." Sadly true. Nonetheless, shouldn't adults protect childhood innocence where they can, rather than moving in concert with the culture's hyper-sexualizing pace?

To argue that young people are growing up sexually no faster today than yesterday is to ignore the statistics. Casual sex, out-of-wedlock pregnancies, sexual diseases—all have exploded in the past few decades. The forces driving this cultural decay are manifold, but an inarguable one is the downward age plunge of opposite sex titillation.

The question is not, "Does your son notice girls?" Of course he does. The question is, "At what speed do you want your son to act on his awareness? At society's? Or at yours?"

Much of the pressure on you comes because you want a slower pace than the new norm. Your son will push on you; you can expect that. What he sees—besides all the cute girls—is a whole crowd of grown-ups who don't think as you do. And these adults, parents even, exert pressure on you. The key to standing strong is to stand on reality: You are the parent; these decisions are yours, not the group's. You know your son best. You know the morals you wish to teach.

To lower the crowd's pressure, you could move with their flow. Less pressure, however, is no sign you're acting wisely. Parenting by moral consensus is not a good way to parent. The consensus that matters here is yours and your spouse's.

I'll bet you have more allies at your son's school than it appears. Other parents would like to get their kids off society's sexual fast-forward but are too intimidated to resist. They admire you, perhaps at a distance, perhaps silently. Your confidence will stiffen their spines.

Cell-Phone Romance

Dear Dr. Ray,
We just discovered that, for the last two months, our thirteen-year-old daughter has been texting a boy from another school. He's become the center of her emotional world.
—Read Enough

Mother, may I take a giant step backward? (Remember "Mother May I?" Back when kids played games face-to-face?) Why does your daughter have a cell phone, and how long has she had one? A cell phone in the hands of a socially impulsive youngster (read "adolescent") calls for trouble.

Parents worry most about the major misuses: sexting, prurient pictures, Internet carousing, minute-by-minute texting. These happen often enough, but as you've experienced firsthand, the potential for social-emotional complications rises with the size of the minute package.

Cell phones can connect kids pretty much to anyone, anytime, anywhere. And the connection is one that the most vigilant parent can't completely monitor. Only when a bad connection becomes clear is the parent motivated to answer the phone trouble.

This is not for me to say, "I told you so." For one thing, I never told you so. For another, it's a first step toward solving your dilemma—one that involves not a partial but a wholesale rethinking of your phone terms.

No doubt your daughter sees her phone as her love line to her boyfriend as well as her indispensable peer link. "How can I talk to my friends without my phone? That's how everybody talks now! I might as well forget about having any friends."

Wow! Social isolation is just a dead battery away. Do you forbid your daughter to speak to her friends face-to-face? Are there real live humans at her school? Do you still have—gasp!—a land phone line? Carrier pigeons? Is any one of these person-to-person type interactions off-limits to your daughter? OK, the pigeons do need some training.

So why does the cell phone drown out her every other mode of communication? Because it's peer approved, 24-7 accessible, and private—all at the top of a thirteen-year-old's most valued list.

Bad news and good news. The bad news: Your daughter believes she has a strong emotional link with this young boy. I mean, how could she not after ten-thousand-plus text messages? For most kids, a mere five thousand adds up to a techno-marriage.

The good news: Pulling the phone's plug—er, charger—could allow this romance to drop from loss of signal, especially since the kids do not have everyday contact at school. Of course, this is assuming your daughter doesn't have unlimited access to e-mail, an iPod, a Twitter account, My Face (or whatever it's called). These too need close watch and perhaps even shutdown. Kids are pros at manipulating the wireless world to go where they want with whom, all under their parents' radar.

For a while, your daughter will most likely commandeer the phone of any friend who agrees that you are total Pony Express throwbacks. Which would include pretty much anyone her age. Still, without her own handheld device, her contact time will decline. And her phone boyfriend may seek other contacts: eighth-grade girls with no phone limits whatsoever.

Are you blocking the problem but not resolving it? I don't know. (I am a highly trained communications professional.) The answer depends upon your daughter's level of attachment, her resentment at being denied her supposed rights, her ingenuity at circumventing your blockade, and the boy's perseverance. Even so, most premature romances require an uninterrupted connection. Without it, one or both parties hang it up.

Many so-called experts would caution against pulling the phone. (Probably most don't have teenagers.) They would intone about the fruit forbidden, the futility of trying to cool youthful feelings, the invitation to sneakiness, and damage to the parent-child relationship. Any of these can be a complication, but what is your alternative?

Persuasion? "Honey, don't you think you're a little too young to be this involved with someone? Do you really know this boy? Do his parents know about you two?" Adolescents would have a range of comebacks to these queries, but most could be summarized with "No, Yes, and Yes."

Do parents allow a child's risky behavior to continue for fear of her reaction at their stopping it? Once a youngster has set a course, must a parent watch it persist, hoping it passes without untoward consequences? Sometimes kids force parents to take a stand that creates static in the short-term but reduces it in the long run.

Your daughter's text-bonding raises a problem. It also signals a much broader question: Why a cell phone at her age?

Socialized? By Whom?

Dear Dr. Ray,

I'm a homeschooling mom of four. If I'm asked one more time, "What about their socialization?" I think I'm going to say something real unsociable.
—Silent So Far

You're on the receiving end of the number-one mantra aimed at homeschooling parents. The question sounds beyond question, but it can be debunked from many directions.

Homeschooled kids are neither raised nor educated on Saturn. Most have brothers and sisters; many have several. Most live in neighborhoods full of people, who talk to them even. Typically they are active with other homeschoolers through field trips, courses, and co-ops. Their world is not a social vacuum.

At a large homeschooling conference, Bill Bennett, the former Secretary of Education, was asked for an answer to what homeschoolers call the "s question." He succinctly replied, "Socialization to what?" Meaning, the word *socialization* has little meaning without defining what kind of socialization?

When I'm asked the "s question," I ask back, "What do you mean?" (Isn't that just like a shrink?) Do you mean the teaching of good conduct, morals, and character? That is, and always has been, the foremost responsibility of parents. Or do you mean learning the social rules of twenty-five same-aged kids? Maneuvering through the peer culture is a skill, to be sure. It is, however, only a sliver of what could be labeled as socialization.

Many parents homeschool because they do indeed want to be their children's primary socializers. They wish to raise their kids at their moral pace and not that of the peer group. They don't consider the crowd a guide to good living. So when asked, "What about their socialization?" they reply, "That's exactly why I'm homeschooling."

An argument raised is, "Children need to learn how to get along with all kinds of people. They need to experience the push and pull of social negotiating."

True, but how are they best equipped to do that? From peers, whose influence may be either pro-socializing or de-socializing? Or from adults, who just might know more about qualities like tolerance, kindness, and responsibility? To be sure, socialization does take place in all kinds of settings. The essence of any social-ization: When, by whom, and how?

For nearly all of human history, across nearly all cultures, there was no such thing as universal childhood education. In this country, the movement is barely three lifetimes old. How then were children socialized prior to the advent of same-aged peer groupings? Did they lack something in their emotional develop-ment? Were they psychologically stunted? Did they lose out on a key piece of childhood well-being?

In fact, research analyzing the social development of home-schooled youngsters offers several conclusions. As a group, the self-images of the homeschooled is as healthy, or more so, as their schooled counterparts. They are more likely to be civic minded, spending more time in volunteer activities. They report a higher level of overall contentedness. So if one defines the term *socializa-tion* more specifically, it seems that homeschoolers do quite well.

Full disclosure: My wife has homeschooled all of our children for nearly twenty years. (She can now kick tail on *Jeopardy*.) I too have done my share of homeschooling. For example, some years ago, one of the little ones dropped a pencil, and I picked it up for him.

My positive view of homeschooling does not imply a negative view of broad-based education. Many fine parents, teachers, and kids are involved in public and private schools. My intention is to knock flat the most common, and the most baseless, objection leveled at homeschooling. It is to defend those who choose that option. These parents are typically involved and conscientious. They are not prone to unwittingly shortchanging their children's overall adjustment.

P.S. My wife graded this for content and grammar. I got a C+/B.

Section Eight

Feelings of Failure

The number-one desire of faith-filled parents is to pass the faith on to their children. Their hope is that their children will embrace that faith throughout childhood and beyond.

So it is with deep distress and no little sense of guilt that a parent watches her child suspect, neglect, or reject much or most of his childhood beliefs. The self-doubt and second-guessing disrupt not only her inner peace but her ongoing relationship with her children, particularly those turned adult.

While all things church may not be unfolding as Mom or Dad expected, that doesn't mean they are at fault. It also doesn't mean the story is over.

Talk the Walk

Dear Dr. Ray,
I've always believed that my actions speak louder than my words. So, as the saying goes, rather than talk religion, I've chosen to walk religion. My kids are nine and thirteen, and I'm not sure they're walking behind me.
—Speechless

The following saying has long been attributed to St. Francis: "Preach the gospel always, and if necessary, use words." In fact, St. Francis never said that. He was a preeminent preacher. The power of his words derived from the power of his actions. The two moved in inseparable tandem. One reinforced the other. Alone, each would not have carried the same weight.

Practice what you preach; walk your talk; values are caught, not taught; children learn what they live. These are all worthy phrases, with a large measure of truth. But they don't speak the full truth.

Most people—"people" includes kids here—are indeed more influenced by another's behavior than by their speech. If one picture is worth a thousand words, then images of good living are worth many thousands of words. Actions that don't match my words, to be sure, hollow out those words. I could be tagged a hypocrite. This is unarguable, yet it needs to be expanded.

Actions alone are not necessarily sufficient. Words are important to the message.

My first assumption: You are older than your children. As such, your moral conduct may be more obvious to you than to them. Put another way, it takes moral maturity to draw good lessons from what one sees in others. A nine- and a thirteen-year-old are still growing into this maturity. For that matter, so are many adults.

Second assumption: Your kids are human. As such, their nature is fallen, bent toward self-interest. Yes, they can observe your exemplary behavior, assuming they are paying attention. Interest in your example, however, collides with their self-interest. While pulled toward emulating you, they are also pulled toward their own wants.

Third assumption: You are human. You too have a fallen nature, always ready to sabotage your best intentions to present a bright moral light. Even the holiest of saints know their light can flicker. Do you always act with moral consistency?

I assume your behavior is overall quite admirable. But does it ever resemble that of a nine-year-old or, worse, a thirteen-year-old? Such is the state of our existence this side of heaven. Try as you might, your fallen nature intrudes and sends your kids, as the psychologists term it, "mixed messages." At which they aren't likely to think, "Gosh, Mom is so good almost all the time. But she's only human, and every so often she slips. I understand. I too have that trouble."

A child's natural bias is to interpret a parent's moral inconsistencies in his favor. Just ask any parent who—after forty straight days of unrattled, loving demeanor in the face of adolescent eye rolls and "Yeah, rights"—finally responds with her own surliness. Will she be lovingly met with, "Oh, Mother, I'm so sorry I've pushed you to your limit these past forty days. You are a walking, talking saint to have endured so long"? Or will she be charged with, "See, you're always telling me to show you respect, but you don't show me any. If you want respect, you have to give respect"?

Some twenty years ago, I returned to the Church, determined to act in moral concert with my beliefs. I don't know if people haven't been paying attention all these years or if I'm not as obliviously holy as I think. Either way, I'm still waiting to hear, "Dr.

Ray, I've been watching you for some time now, and I've been so moved by your moral witness. Can you please tell me the basis for it?"

When the opportunity presents itself, I must be ready to talk my faith too. Without a willingness to offer the reasons underlying my conduct, I could be viewed, at best, as a nice guy. God wouldn't get any of the credit.

Speak openly with your kids about why you live the way you do. It's not that you're merely trying to be a good mom. It goes far deeper than that. It all flows from your relationship with Christ.

Words by themselves don't teach durably. Actions by themselves are more potent than words. However, for maximum teaching power, you need words and actions, both moving in the same direction. To rephrase whoever said it: Preach the gospel always, and make sure your walk matches your talk.

Prayer Aware

Dear Dr. Ray,

My kids—ages six, nine, and twelve—all drift off during family prayers, more so if we go past a minute or two. I worry I'm not getting through to them.

—*Talking to Myself*

I'm assuming "drift off" refers to their heads, not their bodies. If a child wanders off physically, it's not likely his brain will stay put, unless he can bilocate. (If this is the case, I don't think you need be too concerned about the quality of his prayer life at this point.)

G.K. Chesterton, the Catholic philosopher and author, said, "If a thing is worth doing, it is worth doing badly."[6] Applying that to prayer, we can say that, in itself, prayer is worthwhile, so one shouldn't refrain from prayer because he doesn't pray perfectly. Even when the mind isn't one with the words, the heart can be well aimed.

That your children aren't always one with you in prayer is not usually a sign of poor parenting. Their distractions may be due more to age than to disposition. The relationship is pretty basic: Young equals little prayer perseverance. The opposite isn't necessarily true: Older doesn't automatically equal more prayer perseverance. The human mind, even the most mature, retains its proclivity to meander.

Over the years, I've prayed many rosaries, most after I married my wife. Her prayerfulness has pulled me along. Were I to gather all my good rosary prayers, I think I could total maybe between ten and twenty full rosaries. And I've been older than your kids for a long time now.

When our ten children all were under age thirteen, prayer time (and almost any other time) was marked by chaos. During family rosary, we sat in a circle—albeit one that kept shifting—as each of us took a turn to pray one prayer. More times than I care to count, when my turn came, I wasn't sure exactly where we were. Did I need to say another Hail Mary, or was it a Glory Be? Whereupon five or six children and one wife would snicker and compete to correct me. How suddenly they all became so prayer aware!

It's tempting to read a youngster's sloppy attention as irreverence or worse, a flimsy conscience. Often it's neither. It's sloppy attention. Further, a child can be childish in prayer yet beyond his years in morals. Expect time—measured in years, not months—to bring better prayer perseverance. And pray that your children all find prayerful spouses.

Can you take steps to expand your kids' prayer consciousness now? I pray so. Arrange the seats. You know which children make an irreverent mix. If the six- and nine-year-old amuse, distract, or plain agitate one another, don't put them on the same couch. Sit between them, or would that ruin your concentration as well as any remaining sense of piety? Can they pray from separate rooms via intercom?

Stop the action. Cease praying until the kids hear the quiet as their signal to refocus. Silence can speak loudly to regain attention.

And if it doesn't? Go audible: Clear your throat, snap your fingers, call the child by name, pray a little more loudly, set off the smoke alarm. Whatever you do, avoid multiple words or lengthy reminders. Too much talk can pull everybody off track, even more than the kids do.

Rotate turns. Structured devotions—the rosary, the Chaplet of Divine Mercy, litanies—lend themselves naturally to this. It's much harder to drift while speaking than while listening.

Ask the daydreaming or disruptive child to pray, even if "out of turn." My high-school government teacher, Mrs. Houser, called on students who looked most mentally distant. (For months I heard my name so often that I thought I was her pet.) This tactic can nudge the daydreamer back into the flow. It could also arouse his sister to complain, "How come he gets more prayers than me?" Kids become hyper alert at any hint of personal injustice.

As an aside, by March in Mrs. Houser's class, I had mastered the ability to look attentive while being inattentive. My wife caught on to me by our second date.

Know when to quit. Prolonging prayer sessions to compensate for weak cooperation often leads to weaker cooperation. Longer is not necessarily better or holier. Even in prayer, the law of diminishing returns can apply. You might want to reserve some prayers for another time.

Are you still with me?

Asking Adolescent

Dear Dr. Ray,

My sixteen-year-old son is arguing with me about God, the Church, and some of her moral teachings. He says he wants to believe but is too confused.

—Needing Answers

My grandmother emigrated from Italy at age eight. Her family settled into a semi-cloistered Italian-Catholic neighborhood. Her parish was St. Anthony's, also the parish of a young girl named Rita Rizzo. Rita later came to be known as Mother Angelica, the foundress of the EWTN Global Catholic Television Network.

St. Anthony's was at the center of Momo's religious and social life—probably Rita Rizzo's as well. Catholic identity was planted early and remained. If the Church said it, it was so. If Momo had a question, the priest had an answer. Her faith was childlike to the end of her ninety-six years.

So it was for many believers of two or more generations past. Those days, it seems, are in their twilight. The soil for faith is littered with tons of rocks. Our society is aggressively more secular, determined to shove aside God and his ways or to recreate him in line with its ever shifting mores.

It's the younger among us who most confront the widening chasm between childhood belief and the rebellious skepticism of pop culture. What they're taught by family relentlessly clashes with what they're taught by the world around them.

Most likely, your son's questions aren't all his own. Many have originated elsewhere: the media, entertainment, and friends. By a sort of cultural osmosis, others' thinking has seeped into his head. The good news though: Some of the most supposedly enlightened challenges to traditional religion are illogical and shallow, thus easily countered.

A pervasive piece of illogic these days is "I question; therefore, the faith is questionable." No. "I question; therefore, I question." What I personally don't understand about the laws of astronomy could fill Jupiter. Does it follow then that those laws are nonsense or don't exist? To better understand anything, one doesn't stop at his questions; he seeks answers to those questions.

For most of a decade, I wandered from the Church. Questions, doubts too, multiplied for me. And I nagged God: "Help me to believe." I couldn't understand: Why doesn't he increase my faith?

It's beyond question that God knows us infinitely better than we know ourselves. He knew that I couldn't live stuck in my quagmire of confusion. He pushed me to pursue understanding. So I read and listened to and queried others much smarter than I. And I received answers, good answers that had eluded my own narrow thinking.

You say that your son wants to believe. That means he is still open to where his search might take him. Cardinal John Newman, a brilliant Catholic convert of the nineteenth century, said, "Ten thousand difficulties do not make one doubt."[7] That is, honest struggles do not mean abandoned belief. They may mean a desire to believe better.

Welcome all your son's questions—about God's existence, science's challenges, sexual morals, or whatever. Don't let him struggle silently, holding uncertainties inside, wondering if answers exist. His floundering may well be part of his making his parents' faith his own.

One piece of guidance to avoid is: "You just have to believe. You can't think your way to faith." Better to say, "You can't think *all* the way to faith." Faith and reason are not adversaries, despite what modern thinking claims. Yes, faith is beyond reason, but faith is not unreasonable.

What if your son has questions far beyond your ability to answer? Then do what I did: Get help—from books, periodicals, CDs, websites, and apologetics organizations. Some solid Catholic websites offer a search option for specific queries. They also invite calls and e-mails to a staff priest or knowledgeable lay person. A teen's questions may stump you, but they're not going to stump everybody.

The saying is, "It's an ill wind that blows no good." Meaning, something has to be real bad for no one to benefit from it. Your son's confusion may unsettle you, but it will motivate you to learn. In helping him understand better, you too will understand better.

It is no longer my grandmother's world. Challenges to belief are everywhere, but so too are answers.

Two Out of Three?

Dear Dr. Ray,

My sons (ages twenty-nine, twenty-seven, and twenty-three) are all living on their own. Two love the faith they were raised in, and one wants little to do with it. I keep asking myself, "What was different?"

—Mixed Success

I don't know, not without knowing your family anyway. But I do know some general answers that might help you answer your own question.

How a child is raised is just one factor among many in how he matures into and throughout adulthood. To be sure, it's a powerful one, but it must interact heavily with others: his inborn personality, life experiences, associates, absorption of pop culture. And this is the short list.

Yes, your boys were raised in the same family, but that family is not the same for each. It can't be. Each son has different siblings; each was raised by slightly different-aged parents; each likely left home at a different age, with siblings still at home or gone years earlier. The moral and religious upbringing can be similar, but the circumstances around it were ever changing.

Even if you could evenly measure all influences, there is one you can't control: free will. God himself doesn't mess much with that one. When all is said and taught, your children will make their own decisions to move toward or away from God. That reality can be scary for a parent, because there is no guarantee which way a child will decide.

Is teaching the faith little better than a coin flip then? In the end, free will trumps all? In the meantime, watch, hope, and pray?

Not at all. Children raised in the faith more often than not remain in or return to the faith, even if their journey along the way is erratic. And certainly, protecting a youngster from all kinds of godless influences and seductions while his faith takes root will raise the likelihood that he'll choose rightly. When trying to guide a child, however—not something more cooperative, like a rabid Bengal tiger—you do have to recognize that not all of the faith shaping lies in your hands.

Then too, free will is not static. For now, one of your children is ignoring what he was shown earlier in life. By no means does that predict what he will do five, ten, twenty years from now. A beauty of free will: It is always free, always able to correct previous choices, always able to choose for God. Put another way, your son may have chosen for the present, but that choice is not set in stone.

Of course, there is a converse truth here. If you shouldn't take all the blame for one child's faith stumble, you shouldn't take all the credit for another's faith walk. Why some come to God and some don't is a mystery of God's grace. He opens eyes, but those eyes must be open to seeing. You till the soil; God spreads the seeds.

When my kids were younger, as I watched their personalities take very different trajectories, I would joke, "Some of our kids may serve the Church, and some may serve time." So far, no time served. Yet, even if some go astray, that doesn't mean they won't come to serve the Church eventually. People do that.

I Failed Religion

Dear Dr. Ray,
I'm the mother of three children, ages twenty-eight, twenty-three, and fifteen. The oldest has left the Church. The middle one is lukewarm about religion. The jury is still out on the youngest. We so much tried to teach and live the faith. It's hard not to feel like a failure.
—"D–" Parent

Do you live on a farm or in a small town—in 1880? If so, your children's choices are not all that common. For much of Christian history, what children were raised in, they stayed in. The family, clan, or tribe was the unchallenged teacher of beliefs, morals, attitudes—in short, its religion.

Do you live in the U.S.? Have you raised your kids here—in the past forty years or so? Then your experience is not all that uncommon. Surveys confirm your personal circumstances: Young adults are moving away from the Church in distressing numbers.

As we've repeated in this book, the soul-misshaping forces of our irreligious society are everywhere and relentless: television, movies, music, celebrities, academia, advertising. Even when homes try to lock the ugliness out, it can seep in like a vapor and form how someone inside thinks, feels, and believes—often quite counter to what the home is teaching.

Of course, not all young people are so influenced. God's grace, one's free will, personality, and circumstances—all interact to help a child hold tightly to the faith. Nonetheless, many fine parents these days feel what you are feeling: at the least, a profound disappointment, more often failure at not passing on to their offspring a deeper sense of God's presence.

Modern parenting has been muddled by "psychological correctness." That is, there are psychologically correct ways to talk to children, reason with them, discipline them—in short, raise them. Reflect an empathic I-message, apply well-timed positive reinforcement, construct a win-win scenario, design a one-of-a-kind sticker system—and a child can be shaped like clay. A good psychological outcome is foreordained.

While useful for some kids—mostly those who could raise themselves—psychological correctness pulls many well-meaning moms and dads into a futile cycle of tentativeness, second-guessing, and guilt. In the end, it offers no guarantee of a well-adjusted youngster.

Among conscientiously religious parents, a parallel notion is spiritual correctness. While psychological correctness routinely backfires, spiritual correctness routinely works, but not always. It says: Do the spiritual good things—attend daily Mass, say the family rosary, confess regularly, pray together, read the lives of the saints—and you will raise a saint.

Don't misread me. All these are faith-nurturing practices that raise the likelihood of raising a saint. But they are not guarantees of such. And when a parent believes they are, if a saint doesn't ultimately happen, the doubts do: What more could I have done? What did I miss? Where did I fall short? Did I compromise too much with the culture? Was I too Catholic? How could I go so wrong?

Many if not most parents did little or nothing wrong. They imparted the faith as well as they could. Not having God's omniscience, they lived and taught as limited humans.

Suppose, though, that God was beside them every day, whispering precise instructions into their ears. That would guarantee a God-seeking young person, wouldn't it?

At parent presentations, I often ask the audience to answer a series of questions with a simple yes or no.

Is there a God? Yes.

Is Christ God? Yes.

Was he sinless? Yes.

Could he perform miracles? Yes.

Did he have a perfect understanding of human nature? Yes.

Slowly and deliberately, I then ask: Could he get most people to follow him?

At this, a pensive silence drifts through the group, then they answer, no. My last question: "If the God-man himself didn't convert most, why do we think we can do better?"

In the television miniseries *Jesus of Nazareth*,[8] Mary Magdalene meets Jesus in the garden immediately after the Resurrection. He instructs her to go and tell his disciples that he is risen. Upon arriving at the room where the apostles are hiding, Mary Magdalene, barely able to contain herself, reports, "He is alive. I saw him. He told me to tell you."

Mary receives a flat stare from St. Peter and a "women's fantasies" comment from St. Thomas. Whereupon she erupts, "Was his death a fantasy? I saw him die." Regrouping, she finishes, "He told me to tell you, and I have done so." Slamming the door, she storms away.

The scene offers a lesson for godly parents. Jesus told you to raise your children in the faith, and you have done so. Now it is their life and their free choice to believe. God asks us to be faithful, not necessarily successful.

Though you have no assurance that all your devoted years will add up to a religious young adult, you do have other assurances. One, the more faithful a parent, the more likely the kids will follow. And two, of those who leave or outright reject the faith, some will one day return, often more believing than ever. They were given truth to return to.

So you've given yourself a D–, but the semester is far from over.

New-Time Religion

There's a new brand of agnostic thinking on the rise. The old brand said, "I don't know if God exists, so I might as well live as I please." The new brand says, "God exists, but he thinks a lot like me."

This new brand allows room for its adherents to believe religious- and psychological-sounding clichés that serve the self. And to the extent that others hold to that line of thinking, I am validated. The numbers say so.

With a little scrutiny, the most popular of trendy religious notions will unravel, leaving room for more godly thinking.

Spiritual, Not Religious

Dear Dr. Ray,

My sister has little to do anymore with the Catholic faith, in which we were both raised. When the subject comes up, she says, "I'm spiritual, not religious." What do I say?

—The Religious Sister

Some declarations multiply because they soothe the human psyche at many levels. One, they sound smart. The words alone seem to offer both a pithy and a profound insight into the human condition. Two, they sound superior. What the speaker professes is a "more genuine, enlightened" way to be. Three, they sound self-evident, beyond dispute. They need no analysis as to how much sense they really make.

At their core, in fact, such declarations are platitudes—full of superficial appeal but with little substance. They are verbal viruses that spread rapidly through the cultural body, because they suit the self.

People who seek my counseling often introduce themselves with broad labels. "I'm a passive person." "My spouse is aggressive." "My child is stubborn." To move therapy forward, I must put specifics to the generic. "What exactly do you mean by *passive*? Give me some day-to-day examples." "What, in particular, makes you think your child is stubborn?" In other words, I pursue the what, where, and how of the descriptions. Only then can I get a picture of the why.

When your sister proclaims, "I'm not religious, I'm spiritual," she's relying on two words that beg for clarification. So, like a good therapist, ask her, "What do you mean by *religious*?" "If you were religious, what would you be like?" "What is your image of someone who is religious?"

Similarly, seek her meaning of *spiritual*. "What makes a person spiritual?" "Are there different kinds of spiritual?" "How does being spiritual show itself?"

Don't argue or jump on contradictions. Your intent is to hear and understand just how your sister is using those words. In explaining herself to you, she may also explain herself to herself. Sometimes, only by saying things out loud do we hear whether or not we make sense.

If your sister is defining these two words as many do, she's doing so quite narrowly. For example, to her, *religious* may mean "following rules." Not only that, but following rules made by people she considers hypocritical or judgmental. Or *religious* may imply rote, unthinking actions with little heart behind them.

Spiritual, to her, is the loftier word. It speaks of a connection, however loose, to another power, perhaps a higher one. What's better, the power commands little obedience to traditional morals or worship.

Spiritual is among the mushiest of words in the lexicon. It can mean whatever one wishes it to mean. The spiritual one sets his own terms; therefore, he follows them to the letter.

Suppose I announce to my wife, "Honey, from this point forward, I want to be more 'marriage minded' and less married. I think the expectations and structure of marriage are impediments to our true selves. Let's not stifle our relationship with rules. As long as we think lovingly about one another, we don't have to do all the nitty-gritty of actual loving."

Pretty much, I would declare myself free from the active love, responsibilities, and yes, sacrifices crucial to a good marriage. Come to think of it, more people do now seem to want the marriage mind without the marriage. But somehow, I don't think my wife would be enamored with this philosophy.

"I'm spiritual, not religious" is what logicians would call an either-or proposition. That is, one is either spiritual or religious but not both. To a believer in the God of the Bible and his plan of salvation, *religious* and *spiritual* represent a both-and proposition. They exist together, part of the same reality. Religion puts the substance to the spiritual. It defines worship and morality. The words overlap so much that they are nearly interchangeable.

Maybe the next time your sister says, "I'm not religious; I'm spiritual," you can ask, "Can someone be both religious and spiritual?"

Am I Good or What?

Dear Dr. Ray,

My brother no longer pays much attention to the Catholic faith in which we were both raised. He declares, "I'm a good person. That's how God will judge me." In fact, he is a pretty decent guy.
—Just OK Brother

Several decades ago, some expert types advanced the theory that a positive self-image is a key to psychological adjustment. A tsunami of purported benefits follows in the wake of thinking well of oneself—academic success, achievements, better relationships, inner peace. Likewise, the negatives recede—self-doubt, social conflicts, unhappiness, even legal troubles. On paper, it all sounded good. Raise self-esteem, and you raise the desirables of life and lower the undesirables.

Reality is an accurate judge of theories and notions. Over time, the self-esteem movement has seen most of its predicted benefits unravel in the face of researched scrutiny. Put bluntly, self-esteem isn't related to a whole lot.

Even so, faith in the need for high self-esteem has locked itself into the popular mind-set. "You can't like others if you don't like yourself." Children early on are taught the mantras: "I'm special." "No one else is like me." "I'm one of a kind." (Stickers and trophies for everyone!)

At one level, Christians would agree with such self-assessments. Every person indeed has worth, inherent and infinite, because every person is made in God's image. True self-esteem, however, comes from divine declaration, not human.

Some years ago, a survey presented a list of high-profile people and asked respondents, "How likely are these people to go to heaven?" The number-two vote getter was Oprah Winfrey, with

66 percent of people believing she was heaven bound. Only Mother Teresa, at 79 percent, out-polled her. Eighty-seven percent of respondents, however, believed they themselves were likely to see heaven. Conclusion? Most people think they are as holy, or more so, as Mother Teresa.

The critical question is: Who defines what is good? If I do, why wouldn't I be in Mother Teresa's saintly league? I'm the judge. I set the bar, one that is on a level with how I'm living. My standards are as credible as God's.

Does civil society define what good is? I don't cheat, steal, or lie (not that often anyway). I obey most laws, pay my taxes, and am a faithful spouse and a good father. I even get to church once in a while. Overall, I'm a good citizen. My morals are in line with what society and the law say is acceptable.

Perhaps, but society and the law reflect the reigning and ever-shifting standards of the culture, which may or may not reflect God's never-shifting standards. Abortion is legal and approved by half the population, much more in some cases. Does that make it a moral good? Premarital sex, out-of-wedlock pregnancies, even adultery have pretty much become modern acceptances. Judging by the numbers, are they now morally OK? Are they no longer sins that can taint one's goodness?

"I'm a good person" routinely leaves unsaid, "by comparison." If I do less bad than others do, I'm better, relatively speaking. This is the "I'm not on drugs" measure. Given what others are doing or what I could be doing and am not, I look pretty good. God should be grateful.

If God assessed goodness as humans do, most of us would be on fairly solid spiritual ground. Instead, he's made it abundantly clear that we are all sinners in need of his salvation, mercy, and grace. Not that we are bad people. Quite the contrary, we are infinitely valuable souls. Still, God wants us to be good by his terms, not ours.

Too much self-interest clouds my judgment of my own self-worth. It's worth repeating: Real self-esteem comes from God's judgment, not mine.

Ask your brother a few questions next time he asserts that God will approve of his life conduct on Judgment Day. Who decides what is good? Do you believe that everything society declares as good really is? Where would you and God disagree about what is good? Does God judge us on what we call good or on how much we love him and others? Jesus says no one can be good apart from him; are you saying your goodness comes from him?

The final word comes from our Lord. When addressed as "Good Teacher," he answered, "Why do you call me good? No one is good but God alone" (Mark 10:17, 18).

Good Enough for Me

Dear Dr. Ray,

What can I say to a twenty-one-year-old who insists on living how he wants and tells me, "God loves me the way I am"?
—*Love Him*

Tell him two things: Yes, he does; no, he doesn't. As the preachers preach: God loves us as we are, but he loves us too much to leave us as we are.

Your son is right, but not in the way he thinks. God does love him, with his sins and all. God loves him because God is love. His love is unconditional: It does not rise and fall with your son's conduct. God loves him not because of how he acts but because of who he is—a child of God.

So tell your son, "You're absolutely right. God does love you." Then follow with, "You're absolutely wrong too. God doesn't love the wrong that anyone does." His nature can't embrace sin. And God defines sin; we don't.

Draw a parallel. Tell your son that, as his mother, you love him, no matter what, always. But you could never love or accept anything he does that could hurt him. If he's living in ways that are foolish, self-destructive, or wrong, how could you love that? How could you want that for him? That wouldn't be love; it would be misguided, blind emotion.

Your son proclaims, "I don't think I'm doing anything wrong." No doubt he doesn't, or he's trying to convince himself that he doesn't. (Never underestimate the morals you laid down for years, likely still buried somewhere deep within him.) I may proclaim, "I'm talented enough to play major league baseball." Indeed, I can proclaim all sorts of things, all real in my head. That doesn't mean they are real.

The modern mind has taken the phrase "Don't judge me" to an absurd extreme. Not only do people bristle at anyone's judging their conduct as right or wrong; they don't like having God do it either. As they see it, he needs to accept who they are, and that includes what they do. God is no longer Lord of the universe. He is an indulgent uncle who smiles and nods permissively at how his nieces and nephews behave, whenever and however. That's a comforting image. It's not real. It's one of our making.

"God loves me the way I am" is one of a long list of self-created God qualities. Another is "God wants me to be happy." Yes, he does, if that means living the way he knows is best, as he designed us. He doesn't want me to be happy if *happy* means sinning. Chasing sin to find contentment is like playing with a scorpion. It's only a matter of time.

"God understands me." Of course he does. He understands us infinitely better than we understand ourselves. Most of us spend our whole lives trying to see ourselves more clearly, and even so, our vision is clouded, blurred even, by strong self-interest. Because God understands me doesn't mean that he agrees with me.

"God knows my heart." True, he knows my innermost being. He also knows when and how my heart may be misleading me, especially away from him. For many people, *heart* is another word for feelings. And feelings are notoriously fickle guides for living a moral life. Because I feel something is right and good doesn't mean it is. God is the judge of right and good, not my heart.

All this may sound sensible to you. How could your son disagree? Because right now, he may just want to live his way, and his rationale is "God loves me the way I am." He may not totally believe it, only enough to pacify any conscience vibrations.

When trying to reason with your son, you'll likely meet defensiveness. He's protecting his decisions and himself. Nevertheless, don't believe you failed at reaching him. Bits and pieces of what you say could sneak in and sit for later rethinking.

That's pretty much the way most of us change our minds and lives—bit by bit for the better.

Misdirected Wrath

Dear Dr. Ray,
I've heard Christians say, "I'm mad at God," after something bad has happened to them. That has always bothered me, but I'm not sure why.
—Upset

I started college on the engineering track. Mathematics was integral to my course work. Its particular equations have pretty much faded from my mind. A general principle, though, has stuck with me: To correctly solve any formula, one has to have as many equations as one has variables.

God alone knows every single variable involved in any life problem—past, present, and future. He has full knowledge of all the complexities among these variables. Without his help, we barely first-year students in our understanding of life are going to come to some wrong conclusions.

A simple definition of anger: People (or life) are not acting as I would like them to. To be angry at God is to say, "God is not acting as I would like." Either, "I see all this as clearly as God does, and I don't agree with him," or, "I may not understand everything, but what I do understand, I don't like."

Some anger at being mistreated by life is understandable. And since God is the author of all life, the emotion is sometimes directed at him. The emotion is misdirected, however. It arises from a faulty view of God's nature.

God isn't like some ancient mythological deity who flings emotional lightning bolts at people who irritate him. He doesn't play cosmic chess with them as the pawns. God *can't* create evil or wrong, as it is completely contrary to his being. Therefore, to be angry at God is to blame him for something he didn't do. It's getting the main variable in the equation wrong.

"God may not have caused my troubles, but he could have prevented them." God can prevent or stop anything. So why doesn't he? What does he know that we don't?

My son Andrew was born with a cleft lip and palate, requiring several operations. Around age two, he needed blood drawn for an upcoming surgery. Because he was so young, his veins were hard to find. Repeated needle sticks were attempted, as Andrew screamed and struggled against the restraining nurses. He didn't know who his assailants were, and his fear magnified his pain.

Finally I said, "I'll hold him for you." As the nurse continued to probe, Andrew looked up at me—his father and protector—with eyes that said, "Daddy, why are you letting these people hurt me?" All I could think was, "Andrew, if you only knew what I know."

One has to wonder how often God thinks, "If you only knew what I know." Getting angry at God for what we don't know, can't foresee, and barely comprehend is, in a sense, acting like a spiritual preschooler. We believe that what little we see for the moment is all there is or will be to see.

Aiming anger at God may reveal a sense of spiritual entitlement. The thinking runs something like this: "I've been faithful. I've always tried to do what God wants me to do. And then he lets this happen to me." Or to put it more bluntly: "I've played by God's rules. I've kept up my end of the relationship. And this is how I'm rewarded."

Living God's way is its own reward, now and forever. We aren't in a position to set the terms on exactly how life should treat us. That's not what this earthly existence is all about.

Notice, though, that my anger at God is most intense when something bad happens to me. When similar trouble or misfortune befalls another, excepting someone I love deeply, I don't react as strongly. My God-aimed ire is more acute when life hurts me personally.

Anger has both a thinking and a feeling variable. When the feeling rules, we seek someone or something to direct that feeling toward. When no person is seen as responsible for our pain, when faceless life seems to have conspired against us, it is tempting to see God as somehow orchestrating it all. My emotions are telling me so.

That is when good thinking must talk sense into my emotions. God isn't to blame. Nor is he there to stop every pain. Was Jesus angry at his Father for not alleviating his suffering? No, he understood the suffering to be for a greater purpose.

God's infinite goodness is ever ready to bring healing from hurt, good from bad, growth from pain. We have to cooperate with him. And cooperation begins by not being angry at God.

Notes

1. "We might think that God wanted simply obedience to a set of rules: whereas He really wants people of a particular sort." C.S. Lewis, *Mere Christianity* (New York: Macmillan, 1943), p. 77.
2. Fulton Sheen, *Radio Replies: Classic Answers to Timeless Questions about the Catholic Faith*, vol. 1–3, (El Cajon, Calif.: Catholic Answers, 2014), introduction.
3. Sigmund Freud, *The Interpretation of Dreams* (New York: Avon, 1965), p. 647.
4. G.K. Chesterton, *Orthodoxy* (Radford, Virginia: Wilder Publications, 2008), p.13.
5. Josh McDowell, "Rules Without Relationships Lead to Rebellion," Josh McDowell Ministry, http://www.josh.org/video-2/videoplayer/?player=youtube&videoid=Tx1S OiawASw&format=standard&t=Rules%20Without%20 Relationships%20Lead%20to%20Rebellion.
6. The American Chesterton Society, "A Thing Worth Doing," American Chesterton Society, http://www.chesterton.org/ a-thing-worth-doing/.
7. Newman, *Apologia pro Vita Sua* (London: Longman, 1878), p. 239.
8. *Jesus of Nazareth,* TV miniseries, directed by Franco Zeffirelli, 1977.

ABOUT THE AUTHOR

Dr. Ray Guarendi is the father of ten, clinical psychologist, author, public speaker, and nationally syndicated radio and television host. His radio show, *The Doctor Is In,* can be heard weekdays on EWTN Radio and Sirius/XM satellite radio. Dr. Ray's national television show, *Living Right With Dr. Ray,* is entering its fourth season. His many books include *Winning the Discipline Debates* and *Fighting Mad.*